Income, Deprivation and Well-Being Among Older Irish People

By

Richard Layte, Tony Fahey and Chris Whelan

NATIONAL COUNCIL ON AGEING AND OLDER PEOPLE

REPORT NO. 55

NATIONAL COUNCIL ON AGEING AND OLDER PEOPLE
22 CLANWILLIAM SQUARE
GRAND CANAL QUAY
DUBLIN 2

REPORT NO. 55
© NATIONAL COUNCIL ON AGEING AND OLDER PEOPLE, 1999

ISBN 1 900378 13 2

Price £7.00 €8.88

Foreword

Following the publication of *Health and Autonomy Among the Over 65s in Ireland* in 1994, this study of *Income, Deprivation and Well-being Among Older Irish People* represents a further important contribution to the Council's work on the well-being of older Irish people.

In accordance with recent emphasis among policy makers on health gain *and* social gain, the study takes a broad view of well-being, to consider material living standards and deprivation but also mental health, physical health and social interactions.

The study was commissioned in the light of evidence that increases in social welfare pensions were lagging behind growth in average wages. A 1996 study by Callan *et al* showed that income poverty among older people had increased between 1987 and 1994. It therefore seemed timely to study in more detail the situation of older people. Some of the main objectives of this report were to quantify poverty and deprivation among older people and to identify those most at risk in this regard.

The report shows disturbingly, that one in ten older Irish people are at risk of combined income poverty and basic deprivation. Those reliant on the Old Age Non-Contributory pension are at twice the risk on this combination of measures. Female headed households are also at greater risk as are older rural households. Considering solely income, the position of the elderly population has worsened dramatically since 1987, relative to the non-elderly.

As we stand on the threshold of a new millennium and in our current buoyant economic situation, it is unacceptable that so many of our older people are living in these circumstances. It behoves all with an input to government policy to ensure that this situation does not remain a feature in the new century.

On behalf of the Council, I would like to thank the authors of the report, Dr Richard Layte, Dr Tony Fahey, and Prof Chris Whelan for their hard work and professionalism.

I would also like to thank Ms Janet Convery who chaired the Council Committee which oversaw the preparation of this report. For their enthusiasm and dedication, thanks are also due to the members of the Committee: Ms Margaret Burns, Cllr Jim Cousins, Mr Patrick Donegan, Ms Aodhnait Doyle, Mr Frank Goodwin, Ms Catherine Goulding, Prof Hannah McGee, Ms Mary Murphy, Ms Mary Nally, Ms Niav O'Daly, Mr Pat O'Leary, Mr Peter Sands and Mr David Silke.

Finally, the Council would like to thank its Director, Mr Bob Carroll, Research Officer, Dr Nuala O'Donnell and former Research Officer, Mr Frank Houghton who steered the project on the Council's behalf. Thanks are also due to Ms Catherine Mulvenna and Mr John Heuston who assisted in the preparation of the report for publication and to the Council's administrative staff for their assistance throughout the course of the project.

Dr Michael Loftus,
Chairperson, National Council on Ageing and Older People
November, 1999

Authors' Acknowledgements

This report draws on data obtained in the 1987 Survey of Poverty, Income Distribution and Usage of State Services and the 1994 and 1997 waves of the Living in Ireland Survey. We gratefully acknowledge the work of the ESRI's Survey unit and particularly Brendan Whelan, James Williams and Dorothy Watson who were responsible for the survey design, data collection and database creation. We would also like to gratefully acknowledge the substantial contribution of the members of the Consultative Committee set up by the National Council on Ageing and Older People to advise on the study. The members of the Committee read and commented upon a number of drafts of the report. Lastly, we would like to thank Nuala O'Donnell and Bob Carroll for their hard work in organising the meetings of the committee and giving the authors detailed and insightful comments on the report.

Contents

List of Tables and Figures

Tables

Figures

National Council on Ageing and Older People

Comments and Recommendations

Introduction

1. This study represents a further important contribution to the Council's work on the well-being of older people. It follows a study of *Health and Autonomy Among the Over-65s in Ireland,* published in 1994 and a study of *Mental Disorders in Older Irish People: Incidence, Prevalence and Treatment*, published in 1996. The present report updates and expands on much of the material contained in the first-cited study above. This study takes a broad view of well-being, encompassing material living standards and deprivation, but also physical health, mental health and social interactions. All of these factors are important in assessing well-being and living standards. This accords with the recent emphasis among policy makers on the goals of health gain *and* social gain (Department of Health, 1994).

Data

2. The data for the present study come from the 1997 Living in Ireland Survey, conducted by the ESRI. This forms the Irish component of the EU wide European Community Household Panel (ECHP). Earlier surveys are also used to enable trends over a relatively lengthy period be assessed. These earlier surveys are the 1994 wave of the Living in Ireland Survey and the 1987 Survey of Income Distribution, Poverty and Usage of State Services. Both of these surveys were again conducted by the ESRI. All three surveys are highly comparable, those for 1994 and 1997 particularly so. The recency of the 1997 data is an important asset of the study, enabling a relatively up-to-date picture of older Irish people to be painted. Among the other advantages of the data source for the task is the extensive information on income, non-cash benefits and on mental and physical well-being.

3. The sampling frame of the surveys comes from the electoral register. This means that the homeless and older people in long-term care are not covered. Approximately five per cent of the population over 65 are in long-term care. Therefore, as those in long-term care can be thought of as an especially vulnerable group of older people, some of the most vulnerable are not

represented in the survey. This is regrettable but unavoidable in a general national survey.

4. The main focus of the study is on the level and nature of poverty among older people in Ireland, in parallel with consideration of the broader aspects of well-being noted above. Poverty is itself measured in a broad fashion, to include non-cash benefits and reflecting deprivation in relation to societal norms. However, the Council is anxious to stress that non-cash benefits can not be seen merely as income supports but rather relating more to the other aspects of quality of life considered here. This issue will be returned to later.

5. The report considers how the risk of poverty, poor physical and mental health and low levels of social participation vary by household type, age and gender of household head and urban/rural location. As will be discussed below, the particular vulnerability of those living in rural areas and of females emerges.

Policy Context

6. The policy context to the analysis of poverty is the National Anti-Poverty Strategy (NAPS), adopted by the government in 1997 with the aim of addressing the problem of poverty. The NAPS adopts a multi-dimensional approach to the measurement of poverty which incorporates income but also material, cultural and social resources and participation in activities considered the norm for society. While this broad view of poverty is to be welcomed, it appears clear from the report that what is required is not just a multi-dimensional view of poverty but in addition, a multi-group view. Many of the broader poverty reduction targets which the NAPS established are not relevant to the older population, being too heavily focused on labour market and early educational measures.

7. *Therefore, the Council strongly endorses the report's suggestion that the NAPS should be refined to take into account issues more relevant to major sub-groups of the population such as the elderly. While the core measure of poverty as a combination of income and deprivation is relevant to the elderly, issues such as the level of health and social care provision and housing matters pertain much more to their needs than labour market and educational measures.*

8. The report refers to recent commentary from the Combat Poverty Agency that social welfare provision for older people is increasing more quickly than that for other major groups of social welfare recipients, while increases to those on lower social welfare payments may have had a greater impact on poverty reduction (Combat Poverty Agency, 1999). The report also refers to

the fact that the representative of the Minister for Finance on the Pensions Board queried whether the elderly needed more favourable treatment than other social welfare recipients (Pensions Board, 1998). The authors argue that increases in social welfare payments for the elderly can be justified in the context of the government's general poverty reduction targets.

9. *Consistency should be achieved by raising other social welfare payments to the level of Old Age pensions rather than by lowering Old Age pensions. The Council believes that it is essential that social welfare payments are adequate to prevent poverty throughout the lifecycle in order that the population can arrive at older ages in as advantageous a position as possible as regards income, deprivation and mental and physical heath.*

Income Poverty

10. The report shows the high reliance of older people on social welfare pensions. Around 82% of elderly people living alone are reliant on social welfare pensions, a figure which remains high at 74% for two or more elderly living alone. The current compression in the elderly income distribution is striking. The report shows that around 60% of all elderly households live on less than £100 per week, with 90% living on less than £200 per week[1].

11. *The Council strongly concurs with the view that as many people as possible should be encouraged to make second pillar pension provision of occupational and private pensions for themselves, thus ensuring a retirement income proportional to their pre-retirement income and reducing dependency on social welfare payments (Pensions Board, 1998).*

12. *The Council is also concerned at the low numbers of over 65s at work and receiving an income from employment. The Council has previously called for an easing of the structural rigidity in the labour market as regards retirement and again calls for flexible retirement options. Flexible retirement would ease the transition from work to retirement for older people while enabling their skills and experience to be used for a longer period, if they so wished.*

13. The report shows that although the majority of elderly households are not at risk of poverty at the 40% relative income poverty line, the elderly have a greater risk than other household types of being in poverty at the 50% and 60% relative income poverty lines. Over a quarter of elderly households fall under the 50% poverty line and over half fall below the 60% line. These are extremely high and worrying figures.

---

[1] Figures per equivalalised person

Non-Cash Benefits

14. Imputing a cash value to the non-cash benefits received through the Free Schemes lifts a large proportion of elderly households above the 50% line but not above the 60% line, where they have little effect. However, as noted in the report and as will be discussed below, the methodology used most likely over estimates the value of the non-cash benefits. Thus, even with this possible over-estimation, over half of elderly households remain in income poverty at the 60% line.

15. The elderly and particularly elderly females living alone in rural areas have an increased risk of poverty at the 50% line. This is primarily due to the income source of these households with those reliant on Non-Contributory pensions and Widow's pensions at a greatly increased risk, especially those on the Widow's Non-Contributory pension.

16. As noted above, imputing a cash value to non-cash benefits lifts a large proportion of elderly households above the 50% line but not above the 60% line. *However, the Council is concerned that the non-cash benefit schemes should not be seen as purely income supports.* While the Free Schemes contribute to the costs of what can be viewed as necessities in today's society, they have a role above and beyond that of being just income supports. For example, the free travel scheme and telephone rental allowance facilitate important social interactions, enabling older people to keep in contact with family and friends.

17. However, there are many problems with the operation of the schemes. For example, the usefulness of the free travel scheme to older people who live in rural areas where there is little public transport or to those who are ill and immobile can be questioned. Similarly, the telephone rental allowance is of little benefit to older people who do not have a telephone. The Free Telephone Rental allowance does not cover the cost of installing a telephone. Older people who do not have a telephone can not avail of telephone based security and alarm systems.

18. The Council appreciates the difficulties involved in assessing the value of the free schemes to older people. However, it must be emphasised that the methodology used in the report over estimates the value of the schemes to older people who for whatever reason can not avail of the services or who would not have purchased the services provided by the schemes were they not provided free.

Deprivation

19. Considering the risk of deprivation, the elderly are less likely than the general Irish population to experience basic[2] and secondary deprivation. That anyone must experience basic deprivation or an enforced lack of food and clothing in today's society should be unacceptable. The elderly are more likely to experience housing deprivation, with a greater chance of having lower quality housing affected by dampness and structural problems. 11% of elderly households reported having damp walls, floors etc with around 8% reporting a lack of adequate heating and rot in windows and floors. These figures are disturbingly high. In its review of the implementation of the recommendations of the Years Ahead report, (National Council on Ageing and Older People, 1997) the Council made several comments and recommendations with regard to housing issues for older people, as documented by the authors in Chapter 10. These recommendations remain extremely valid and require attention and implementation.

20. The rural elderly face a greater risk of housing and secondary deprivation, while the rural elderly over 75 have a greater risk of basic deprivation. Those in rural households have a greater chance of experiencing dampness and rotting floors and windows than urban households. Females experience greater risk of basic and secondary deprivation. Single households also have a greater risk of housing deprivation after taking into account, age, gender and urban or rural location.

Income Poverty and Deprivation

21. Considering the risk of income poverty at the 60% line and basic deprivation in tandem, a measure of poverty consistent with the NAPS[3] framework, elderly households have a similar risk on this combined measure than non-elderly households, at around 10%. Those reliant on the Old Age Non-Contributory pension are at twice the risk of experiencing poverty on this combined measure. Female headed households are also at greater risk of being in NAPS poverty as are older rural households.

22. These results suggest that the majority of elderly households manage to avoid extremes of deprivation, even given that they have low incomes. This may be due in some part to the role that non-cash benefits play but other factors such as patterns of consumption and levels of expectation may also play a role. However, a figure of 10% experiencing income poverty and

---

[2] Basic – enforced lack of food and clothing; secondary – lifestyle items and consumption indicators; housing – items on housing quality and durables.

[3] Thus, often referred to as "NAPS" poverty.

basic deprivation is still unacceptably high and shows much needs to be achieved.

How has the Situation of the Elderly Evolved over Time?

23. The incomes of the elderly had improved greatly from the early 1970s to the late 1980s. In the early '70s, the elderly had a higher risk of income poverty than any other segment of the population. By the late '80s, the proportion of the elderly in poverty had fallen sharply. Between 1987 and 1997, the risk of income poverty at the 50% line has increased sharply for elderly households[4] (excluding non-cash benefits) while the situation of non-elderly households has remained more or less unchanged. At the 60% level, while the increases in the risk of elderly poverty have not been as sharp, they have been from a much higher base so that a very high 66% of households with heads aged over 74 in 1997 were under the 60% poverty line. There had actually been falls in the proportions of non-elderly under the 60% line between 1987 and 1997[5]. *Thus, considering solely income, the position of the elderly population has worsened dramatically since 1987, relative to the non-elderly.*

24. There has been a reduction in the level of basic deprivation among the elderly, between 1987 and 1997, as with the rest of the population. Levels of secondary deprivation also fell, as did levels of housing deprivation. However, it is important to remember that the elderly experience higher levels of housing deprivation than the rest of the population.

25. These changes mean that at the moment the combined poverty measure or the 'NAPS' measure shows almost similar levels of deprivation and poverty for elderly and non-elderly households. However, this masks the fact that the proportion of households with a head aged over 74 experiencing 'NAPS' poverty grew by 4 percentage points between 1987 and 1997. The situation of younger elderly households worsened between 1987 and 1994 and improved between 1994 and 1997, but did not fall to the level of 1994. By contrast, the situation of non-elderly households improved between 1987 and 1997. These older elderly households whose position worsened are more likely to be composed of elderly females living on their own.

26. With 66% of households with heads aged over 74 experiencing income poverty at the 60% relative line and one in ten of all elderly households in 'NAPS' poverty, much has to be achieved. Older people who have

---

[4] With most of the increase taking place between 1994 and 1997.

[5] The proportion of non-elderly households without children under the 60% line increased somewhat between 1994 and 1997.

contributed so much to the current economic boom can not be forgotten in the distribution of the fruits of success. As described in the main report, the target rate of £100 for the Contributory Old Age / Retirement pension by 2002 will only preserve the income position of older people relative to national average household income. The relative position of recipients will not improve. *Given the current buoyant economic situation, the Council believes that the £100 commitment could be delivered on immediately rather than implemented incrementally over the next three years.*

27. *In general, the Council is of the view that social welfare pensions should be indexed to net average earnings and at such a rate that income poverty for those dependant on social welfare pensions does not become institutionalised.* The Pensions Board in 1998 recommended that the government should aim to increase the Contributory pension to 34% of average industrial earnings over the next five to ten years. The government commitment to £100 by 2002 would fall considerably short of this target, given likely future growth in earnings.

28. *Attention should urgently be given to the lower pension rates, namely the Non-Contributory Old Age pension and the Widow's pensions, both Contributory and Non-Contributory. The Council has previously recommended that the differential between the Contributory and Non-Contributory pension rates should be removed.* As discussed in the report, this would have a large favourable impact on poverty among the elderly, particularly so among females. The fact that the Non-Contributory pension is means tested provides sufficient recognition of the contributory principle, something not achieved by the small differential between the two rates.

Poverty and Older Women

29. The particular vulnerability of older women to poverty and deprivation is clear from the report. Many older women are dependent on the Non-Contributory pension or the Widow's pension. For today's older women, many had no option but to leave the workforce upon marriage and motherhood, given the lack of childcare arrangements, unequal pay and tax arrangements. This was further exacerbated by the marriage bar which forced many women to leave paid employment on marriage. The Homemaker's allowance was introduced in April 1994 and means that time out of the workforce to care for children or an incapacitated person is disregarded when the yearly average contributions for the Old Age Contributory pension are being calculated. The scheme now applies to those caring for children under 12 or disabled or incapacitated people who require continuous supervision. Time spent out of the workforce for these reasons before 1994 is still counted in calculating the yearly average. Thus, this is of little benefit to older people, mainly women, who have devoted time to child-rearing or caring for an incapacitated person.

30. *The Council recommends that the extension of the Homemaker's allowance retrospectively should be considered. This would enable many older women to avail of the Contributory pension, which would be an effective way of alleviating income poverty among older women.*

31. A related issue to the Homemaker's allowance is the individualisation of benefits. *The Council agrees with the recommendation in the Final Report of the National Pensions Board that the pension system needs to incorporate individualisation of payments for qualified adults.* This point was also raised in the Council response to the National Pensions Policy Initiative Consultation document. The 'adult dependants' of persons receiving a contributory social welfare pension should receive an allowance (called an Old Age allowance) in their own right once they have reached pensionable age.

32. This issue is again particularly relevant to women. Given the situation outlined above which today's older women experienced in the workforce, it is unfair that in their old age, they should be treated as dependant. Rather, the contribution they have made in the workforce or in the home should be recognised independently. The Non-Contributory pension has always operated on an individual basis because of the means test.

Physical Health and Material Living Standards

33. The report finds higher levels of chronic illness among older age groups as we would expect. 43.6% of those aged 65 plus reported a chronic mental or physical illness. Chronic illnesses among the elderly appear to hamper their daily activities more than among younger age groups and to have a greater effect on their perceived health status. Almost half of those with a chronic illness also experienced mobility problems. Rehabilitation is vital to those with mobility problems. Currently, access to community care services including occupational therapy, physiotherapy and speech therapy is limited and variable within and among regional health board areas (Ruddle *et al,* 1997). Much remains to be accomplished before appropriate rehabilitation services are in place. At the moment, access to rehabilitation services and community care services in general can depend on the area in which a person lives, which is patently unfair.

34. Basic or secondary deprivation proved to be a strong predictor of ill health and being female is also a strong risk factor. The results on deprivation probably reflect the effect of a long-term lack of resources, rather than a short-run effect. Again, the disadvantaged position of women is worrying.

35. The Council believes the link between socio-economic status and health to be vital in terms of our understanding of the well-being of older people. There is much international evidence that life expectancy and health vary with socio-economic conditions within each age group. Nolan (1991), in the Irish context, shows evidence of a strong relationship between social class and physical illness in each major age group. *Alleviating income poverty and deprivation also fights against ill-health in older people, which in the long-run would be efficient from a fiscal stance.*

36. Older people showed a higher degree of usage of medical services than the population in general, with a quarter of the over 65s having been admitted to hospital in the previous year. However, the survey showed that a considerable proportion at 30% lack a medical card, giving free access to medical services. A disturbingly high 11% of the elderly have neither a medical card nor private medical insurance. Those without a medical card had a substantially lower number of visits to the GP in the year before the survey than those with a medical card. As noted by the authors, this suggests that some among the 30% of elderly people without a medical card may be restricted to some degree in their GP visits. This has obvious negative implications for illness prevention and health promotion. Older people should receive every encouragement to avail of timely care from their GP. This can reduce the need for hospital admission on an acute or long-stay basis.

37. *The Council welcomes, in principle, the provision introduced in the 1999 budget to double the income guidelines used to establish medical card eligibility over the next three years. However, the three year period seems unduly long. Given the importance of medical cards in health promotion and illness prevention, the Council believes that the income guidelines should be doubled immediately, enabling many more older people to become eligible for a medical card.*

Psychological Health and Material Living Standards

38. An analysis of the psychological health profile of those aged over 65 using the General Health Questionnaire showed that women were more likely to have higher levels of psychological distress than men, with a positive relationship between ageing and levels of distress, for both men and women. There is a strong link between levels of distress and levels of chronic illness with the impact of illness on mobility also an important factor. The link between mobility problems and psychological distress is higher among the elderly than the rest of the population.

39. The link between resources and psychological distress was also clear. Controlling for having a chronic illness, being income poor or deprived increases the likelihood of experiencing psychological distress. As poverty, deprivation and having a chronic illness often go hand in hand, these three variables together strongly increase the risk of psychological distress.

Social Interaction and Participation

40. The results of this report concur with those of earlier work which suggested that the elderly were not at any greater risk of social isolation than the general population (Fahey and Murray, 1994). Irish over 65s are less likely to live alone than older people in other countries and more likely to live among kin. Single elderly people appear not to have lower levels of interaction with people outside the household than those who do not live alone.

41. The link between income and social participation was complex but showed a positive relationship between income poverty and the frequency of contact with neighbours, although this effect reduced with age. A negative relationship was found between income poverty and contact with friends and family, after age 69. This suggests that if resources allow, elderly people will replace contacts with neighbours with contacts with friends and family, when age permits.

42. However, for elderly in rural areas, there was a significant decrease in the proportion having daily contact with friends, neighbours and relatives. Rural elderly also had lower participation rates in clubs and organisations than their urban counterparts. The same is true for females in comparison to their male counterparts. The poor provision of public transport in rural areas is undoubtedly a critical factor. *Public transport services in rural areas must be expanded.*

43. A co-ordinated approach across government departments and service providers is required. As far back as 1986, the National Council for the Aged called for the innovative development of rural transport, building on existing services, voluntary effort and integrating where appropriate the private / commercial sector. Specific examples of possible innovative developments include greater and more flexible use of school buses, post buses and health board vehicles. An evaluation of a pilot rural community transport project in North West Connemara showed that these co-ordinated schemes can be extremely successful (Lightfoot, 1995). Their wider application must be considered. *The Council strongly urges the government to formulate an overall policy for rural transport services. In the meantime, implementation of the innovative schemes described above would improve matters considerably. One short-term measure which would greatly improve the situation would be the use of vouchers which would enable older people* *to use private sector bus operators and taxis in rural areas. This would offset to some extent the fact that the free travel scheme is often of limited use in rural areas.*

44. In urban areas, problems also exist. Free travel is not available between 7 am and 9.45 am and between 4.30 pm and 6.30 pm. As many medical appointments for older people are in the morning, older people may not be able to avail of the free travel scheme to carry out these essential journeys. *The Council believes that older people should be able to use free travel for this purpose and suggests that presentation of a medical appointment card should allow the older person avail of free travel for the related journey.* In rural areas, health boards should consider ways in which they can facilitate older people attending for medical appointments. Another problem in both urban and rural areas is that older people with a free travel pass can not reserve a seat on a train. The Council believes that this situation must be reviewed.

Community Care Services

45. While the whole range of health and social care services are obviously vital to the well-being of older people, the Council has had a particular long-standing concern that community care services be further developed to meet the needs of older people. These services enable older people remain at home in dignity and independence, one of the stated objectives of *The Years Ahead.* They also may delay and overcome the need for entry into expensive institutional care. Community care services are crucial to the Department of Health and Children's stated aim of maintaining at least 90% of people aged 75 or more in their own homes, (Department of Health, 1994). The key community care services for older people and their carers are domiciliary nursing, Home Helps, respite services, day care centres and meals services along with occupational therapy, physiotherapy, chiropody, speech therapy and social work services. As noted above, access to these services is limited and variable within and among regional health board areas (Ruddle *et al,* 1997).

46. *The Council has previously called for community care services to be designated as a core service and expanded significantly (National Council on Ageing and Older People, 1997) and again re-iterates this call.* This designation would require the State to provide the services to all those who need them on the grounds of dependency or social circumstances. Clear and universal guidelines for the assessment of eligibility on the basis of need would be established at a national level. The discretionary service that currently exists would be replaced by a transparent and equitable system of service delivery. The services would be underpinned by legislation and appropriate funding. However, because legislation can often restrict the development of services (Mangan, 1997), appropriate legislation should allow scope for new services to be developed and delivered in an imaginative way and room for new initiatives to be taken.

Conclusions and Future Research

47. This report represents a further significant contribution to the Council's work on the well-being of older people. Among the most disturbing aspects of the report is the particularly vulnerable situation of the rural elderly and females which emerges. The fact that 10% of the elderly population and indeed the same proportion of the total population experienced 'NAPS' poverty or income poverty and basic deprivation in 1997 should be unacceptable to everyone. The importance of adequate resources and opportunities throughout the lifecycle is crucial if these figures are to be permanently reduced.

48. The Council believes that social welfare payments will always be of great importance to the well-being of a large proportion of the older population. It is vital that the government recognises that the commitment under the *Action Programme for the Millennium* to a rate of £100 for the Contributory Old Age/Retirement pension by 2002 will likely only preserve the income position of older people relative to national average household income and will do little to eradicate poverty.

49. The issues of health promotion and illness prevention can also make a great difference to the quality of life of older people. The Council believes that older people should receive every encouragement to maintain and improve their health status and prevent illness and disability. In this regard, the medical card is of vital importance. The Council believes that the doubling of the income guidelines used to establish medical card eligibility should take place immediately rather than being phased in over a three year period.

50. Community care services are paramount to enabling older people remain at home in comfort and dignity for as long as possible, one of the stated objectives of government policy for older people. If the government are serious about this aim, community care services must be expanded, and soon. If the current inequitable situation continues, this would surely cast doubt on the commitment to this aim.

51. The Council believes that future research in this field should be more closely targeted on those whom the report has shown to be most vulnerable, i.e., females and the rural elderly but also those in the private rented sector and those whom the report did not cover at all, i.e., the homeless, those in long-stay care and elderly travellers. While often small in overall terms, these groups are most likely to be left behind by the current economic boom. Further focused research would help profile their situation and target their needs.

References

Combat Poverty Agency (1999) *Poverty Today Supplement,* April/May

Department of Health (1994) *Shaping a Healthier Future – A Strategy for Effective Healthcare in the 1990s,* Dublin.

Fahey, T. and Murray, P. (1994) *Health and Autonomy Among the Over 65s in Ireland,* Report No. 39, National Council for the Elderly, Dublin.

Mangan, I. (1997) "Equity, Consistency and Comprehensiveness: The Need for a Legislative Framework to Govern the Provision of Essential Services for Older People," in *Conference Proceedings: Review of the Implementation of the Recommendations of The Years Ahead – A Policy for the Elderly and Implications for Future Policy on Older People in Ireland.* Dublin: National Council on Ageing and Older People

Nolan, B. (1991) *The Utilisation and Financing of Health Services in Ireland,* ESRI General Research Series, Paper No. 155, Dublin: ESRI.

The Pensions Board (1998) *Securing Retirement Income,* National Pensions Policy Initiative, Report of the Pensions Board, Dublin.

Ruddle, H., Donoghue, F. and Mulvihill, R. (1997) The Years Ahead Report: A Review of the Implementation of its Recommendations. Dublin: National Council on Ageing and Older People, Report No. 48.

The Stationery Office (1997) *Sharing in Progress, National Anti-Poverty Strategy,* Dublin

CHAPTER ONE

Introduction

Objectives of Report

This report examines the extent and nature of poverty among older people in Ireland and explores policy options for dealing with elderly poverty. Poverty is a complex, often contentious, concept, and there are aspects to the material circumstances of older people which pose particular challenges for the definition and measurement of poverty. The report therefore devotes considerable attention to conceptual and measurement issues and to the particular way these issues relate to the circumstances of older people. Based on its consideration of these issues, the report identifies and explores a range of dimensions in older people's material conditions and draws these together in an attempt to provide a nuanced assessment of poverty among the elderly.

As well as quantifying the numbers of older people whose material standards of living are inadequate, the report also attempts to profile related aspects of their circumstances, principally in regard to physical and psychological health, family situation and social networks. This is in recognition of the interaction between poverty and these other dimensions, the effects of which go beyond purely material need. It also allows for a consideration of policy issues which go beyond the distribution of income and other material resources (though these remain central) and addresses a range of other policy areas which have a direct bearing on older people's quality of life.

There are numerous definitions of quality of life and no single agreed method of measuring it, particularly among the elderly (O'Boyle et al., 1992). However, research suggests that socio-economic well-being and general health are two of the key aspects of an infinite number of possible dimensions (George and Bearon, 1980), to which we could also add social contact and participation as particular concerns of the elderly (Farquhar, 1995). Thus, while not pretending to give a complete account of the quality of life of those over 65, this report does examine the areas shown to have most importance.

The report is based on data from the 1994 and 1997 rounds of the Living in Ireland Survey, a large-scale household panel survey which is the Irish component of the EU-wide Household Panel Survey. This data source focuses particularly on incomes and living standards but includes a great deal of additional information on other aspects of well-being and quality of life.

Key Issues
As a preliminary to the detailed analyses contained in the body of the report, it may be useful at this point to summarise the key substantive issues which arise in connection with elderly poverty and to outline the policy context in Ireland in which these issues need to be addressed.

Trends in Elderly Incomes
The first and most obvious substantive issue concerns elderly incomes. The income position of the elderly in Ireland has fluctuated widely over the last two to three decades. In the early 1970s, data on income distribution indicated that the incomes of the elderly were low and they had a higher risk of income poverty than any other major segment of the population (see Chapter 3 below). By the late 1980s, the incomes of the elderly had improved both absolutely and relative to both those working and other social welfare recipients. The proportion of older people with poverty-level incomes had fallen sharply (Callan *et al.* 1989), though many of the non-poor elderly at that time could be considered as 'nearly poor' in income terms rather than well off. Since the early 1990s, a number of parallel transitions have occurred and their net impact on the income position of older people is not yet clear. Major components of elderly incomes (especially old age pensions) have risen in absolute terms. However, they have done so more slowly than the general rate of growth in the economy, particularly in view of the unprecedented surge in overall economic growth rates which has occurred in recent years.

This raises the prospect that, despite absolute improvement, the relative position of the elderly may have deteriorated to the point where gaps are opening up again between their incomes and rapidly rising income norms for the rest of Irish society. This gives rise to the first task for the present study, which is to update the picture of elderly incomes, locate them in the overall income distribution in Ireland and quantify the extent of income poverty which can be identified as a result.

Non-Income Resources and Elderly Poverty
As long ago as 1972, Ó Cinnéide, in his pioneering examination of poverty in Ireland, asserted that 'the very idea of a poverty line defined only in terms of current income is outmoded: the limitations and anomalies in the idea have been clearly demonstrated by many writers' (Ó Cinnéide 1972, p. 397). Apart from cash incomes, three additional types of resources can be identified which need to

be taken into account in assessing poverty and its impact:

- Asset holdings
- Public social services
- Private benefits in kind

Each of these is relevant to the circumstances of the elderly in Ireland and we will discuss each in turn.

Asset Holdings

As far as assets are concerned, the most important consideration in connection with the elderly are housing and household durable goods, though financial assets are also significant for small numbers of older people (Honohan, 1993). Approximately 90% of the elderly own their houses (with no remaining mortgage in nine cases out of ten) and older people also typically have built up a considerable stock of household durable goods. They draw consumption benefits from these assets, which require little cash outlay. Younger householders, by contrast, are more likely to have to pay a mortgage or rent on their dwellings and to be in the process of purchasing household durables, all of which could absorb large portions of current income. For any given amount of income, therefore, possession of such assets on the part of elderly householders can give them a higher standard of living than one would expect or than is enjoyed by younger householders on similar incomes.

Assets do not always yield consumption benefits in proportion to their value. Many older people, for example, live in houses that are too big for their needs or have valuable features (such as closeness to places of employment) which are irrelevant to their circumstances. They thus can be asset rich and income poor, or wealthy and deprived at the same time. This not only complicates the task of defining and measuring poverty. It also raises a number of policy questions – how far wealth holdings should be taken into account in determining the appropriate level of state support for older people, whether equity release schemes should be developed to enable older people to draw secure income from property assets, whether post mortem claw-backs from older people's estates should be introduced as a means to recover at least part of the cost of expensive public services (such as long-term institutional care), which they may have received in their final years. Questions such as these have become particularly pressing in recent years with the rapid growth in house values and thus in the wealth of homeowners, of whom the elderly account for a disproportionately large share. Widening wealth inequalities which arise from increasing asset values can run counter to inequalities in income and can be structured along generational lines – older generations (who are more likely to be homeowners) benefit most, while younger generations (who are trying to enter into homeownership) lose out. But even among older generations, wealth gaps may widen between the majority who own housing and the minority who do not. In any event, it is evident that for both research and policy on poverty, questions of wealth as well as of income need to be systematically addressed and are so in this report.

Public Social Services
The second type of non-cash resource which is important in the analysis of poverty is public social services, of which, in the case of older people, the most important forms are social housing, a wide range of 'free schemes' targeted on the elderly (free travel, free electricity, free television licence, etc.), and health and social care entitlements. Of the 15 per cent of elderly who are not homeowners, a large number (5.8 per cent of elderly households) rent their dwellings from local authorities at heavily subsidised rents. This reduces the significance of the wealth gap between homeowners and non-homeowners in the elderly population, though it does not eliminate it entirely (particularly on account of the balance of elderly households which are housed in the most exposed housing tenure, private rented accommodation). The majority of the elderly also benefit from 'free schemes' and their monetary value adds significantly to older people's real incomes (see Chapter 3 below for details). Health and social care services, however, are undoubtedly the most important element in public social services for older people, not only because older people are more likely to suffer from illness and disability but also because, even for those elderly who are fit and well, worry about the availability, quality and cost of health and social care services typically looms large in their minds. For many older people, quality of life may be less affected by income levels than by issues such as Medical Card coverage, waiting lists in hospitals, the local availability and accessibility of any of a wide range of medical services, and the cost and availability of social care or long-term institutional care when and if they become frail and dependent.

Private Benefits In Kind
The final broad category of resources which needs to be taken into account in assessing poverty consists of private benefits in kind. In the case of the elderly, these are most likely to consist of intra-family transfers of material and instrumental support. Research in Ireland and in other countries has shown that material transfers between adult generations run overwhelmingly downwards – older people give more to adult children than the other way around – but instrumental support (caring and helping out with regular tasks) in general tends to flow in the other direction, and does so quite decisively when older people become ill or incapacitated. Such transfers, however, occur overwhelmingly within immediate families (between parents or parents-in-law and adult children) and this is significant in Ireland on account of the large proportions of older

people who do not have any families in this sense. Over 20 per cent of the elderly in Ireland never married and have no children (the corresponding proportion in most other western countries is in the range 5-10 per cent). They thus lack the family networks that are an important part of well being for most of those elderly who did marry and have children and which can be a valuable safeguard against certain kinds of poverty and social marginalisation.

Multi-dimensionality of Vulnerability

The multiplicity of resources which can be available to households and which affect their standard of living clearly indicate that disadvantage can be multi-dimensional – households can lack one or more resources and can thus experience vulnerability in any of a number of ways. As an illustration, consider the hypothetical case of two men in their seventies, both of whom receive non-contributory old age pensions, hold medical cards and are entitled to a wide range of 'free schemes' (free electricity, free travel, etc.). The first is a bachelor living in a low-value house in a thinly-populated rural area. He has no car, no close relatives living nearby, he spends long periods alone, the nearest village is two miles away, the nearest major town with hospital and related services is 15 miles away, and there is no public transport. His health and physical mobility are beginning to fail and he is worried about every aspect of his future. The second man is married, lives with his wife and young adult son in a small but pleasant suburban house in Dublin that has risen dramatically in value in recent years. Other grown up children live nearby and he has an abundance of grandchildren whom he sees as he wishes. He has good access to public transport and makes regular use of his free travel pass, his son has a car, he and his wife both enjoy reasonable health, a wide range of social and leisure services are available in the vicinity and he has an active social life. As he depends mainly on his old age pension for an income, he is not well off, and would have difficulty meeting any sudden unexpected expense that might arise. He thus might be counted as poor or near-poor in income terms. However, he is in no sense socially excluded, enjoys his present life and faces his future with equanimity.

These two cases are in a similar position in narrow income terms. However, the first lives a life of considerable impoverishment in the present and severe vulnerability for the future, while the second is embedded in a web of social and material supports and public services which offers both present and future guarantees of at least minimum security and quality of life. The differences between them illustrate the dimensions along which vulnerability can arise and point to the need in the present study to consider factors such as health, family and household circumstances, location and the availability of services in assessing the nature and extent of poverty among older people.

Policy Context

The immediate policy context for the present report is provided by the National Anti-Poverty Strategy (NAPS) which was adopted by the Irish Government in 1997. This is a major cross-departmental initiative which draws on ten years of poverty research in Ireland to define the extent and nature of the problem of poverty and set targets for poverty reduction over the period 1997-2007. It significance lies in the first instance in the commitment of government to address problems of poverty which it expresses. In addition, it is important on account of the broad, multi-dimensional definition of poverty that it adopts. This definition gives official sanction to a view of poverty that refers to 'material, cultural and social resources' as well as income and to the impact which inadequate levels of such resources have on exclusion and marginalisation from normal activities.[1] Furthermore, the NAPS gives substance to this definition through a set of headline targets for poverty reduction which it establishes.[2] As a broad-brush strategy, the NAPS does not address the problem of elderly poverty in any detail, but it does provide a policy framework within which elderly poverty can be explored and policy responses to that problem can be developed. For that reason, the present report links its investigation of elderly poverty as far as possible to the framework provided by the NAPS, while at the same time retaining a concern for the distinctive position of the elderly and the forms of impoverishment to which they are particularly vulnerable.

Other broad aspects of the present context in Ireland are unusually favourable to the development of effective policy for dealing with elderly poverty (Fahey 1997). Exchequer finances are in a very strong position, following the fiscal

---

[1] The full definition is: 'People are living in poverty if their income and resources (material, cultural and social) are so inadequate as to preclude them from having a standard of living which is regarded as acceptable by Irish society generally. As a result of inadequate income and resources people may be excluded and marginalised from participating in activities which are considered the norm for other people in society' (Government of Ireland, 1997. p. 3).

[2] The headline targets on these items adopted in the National Anti-Poverty Strategy are as follows (Government of Ireland 1997, pp. 8-19):

- Over the period 1997-2007, the proportion of the population which is 'consistently poor' (i.e. on low income *and* suffering material deprivation) should be reduced from the range 9-15% to the range 5-10%.

- Rates of completion of second-level education should be raised to 90% in 2000 and 98% in 2007, and avoidable literacy/numeracy problems among primary school children should be eliminated within five years.

- Unemployment rates should be reduced from 11.9% in 1996 to 6% by 2007, and long-term unemployment should be reduced from 7% to 3.5%.

- Living standards and social participation among those living in disadvantaged urban areas (especially with regard to employment) should be raised.

- Improve service delivery in rural areas to ensure that anti-poverty targets are achieved.

correction of the late 1980s and the buoyancy in the economy of the last 3-4 years. Demographic structures are now moving in a positive direction: the population of young adults is growing rapidly, as is the size of the labour force. This is allied to a relatively modest rate of growth in the elderly population, as a result of which the ratio between the elderly and the working population is moving in a strongly favourable direction. This provides a strong underpinning for the financial support of older people for the years ahead[3]. Furthermore, the flat-rate structure and broad coverage of the social welfare pensions system, coupled with the smallness of the gap between contributory and non-contributory pension benefits, amount to something approaching a state provided minimum income guarantee for older people. This income guarantee is not satisfactory in some respects. For example, it does not always provide older people with a retirement income that is proportionate to their pre-retirement wages or salaries (private occupational pensions are now being promoted by public policy as a means to remedy this defect in older people's incomes for the future). However, it does provide a powerful instrument of anti-poverty policy. Social welfare pensions expenditure is in effect directed at the floor incomes for older people, so that any increase in the level of pension benefit translates efficiently into the raising of floor incomes and thus at the reduction of income poverty among older people. In the social welfare pensions system, therefore, public policy has to hand an efficient and effective policy instrument for dealing with one major dimension of elderly poverty – and one which has broad popular acceptance to boot.

Certain aspects of the policy environment are less favourable to the well being of older people, and some of these aspects are of long standing. The most important arise in connection with services for older people, both public sector services and private services which are influenced by incentives (whether positive or negative) arising from the policy environment. The principle that older people should be enabled to 'age in place' and that institutionalisation of frail elderly should be an option of last resort has been enunciated in various forms in Irish policy for all of three decades. However, the services and supports necessary to give effect to that principle have been slow to emerge, have attracted little sense of urgency and are now underdeveloped in Ireland. It often appears that the policy environment is more likely to promote high-cost institutional provision which is inappropriate to many older people's needs than to provide the kind of community-based services that older people really want and need and that may be cheaper on a unit-cost basis. The use of institutional geriatric care rather than

---

[3] The Actuarial Review of Social Welfare Pensions (1997) projects the numbers of elderly to increase from 11% at present to 19% in 2026 and 27% in 2056. Although the numbers at working age will increase in the first two decades of the 21st Century, they may decrease thereafter lowering the ratio of over 65s to those at working age from 4.9 at present to 1.9 by 2056.

21

community and home based care is one example of provision in this area that may be seen as inappropriate. The underdevelopment of home help services, rural public transport and sheltered housing for semi-dependent elderly people (particularly those who do not qualify for the forms of such housing provision which have emerged in the social housing sector) are examples of the failures of service provision which make it difficult for many older people to realise the principle of 'ageing in place'.

Research Approach

The present study cannot give equal coverage to all of the issues which are relevant to elderly poverty, mainly on account of data limitations (the available data, for example, give little information on intra-family transfers of resources to and from older people). However, the available data do contain rich information on many aspects of older people's living standards and quality of life, and the study aims to reflect that richness. Its approach is, first, to focus on elderly incomes, then to explore indicators of deprived living standards among older people and the way these interact with low incomes, and from that to derive estimates of the numbers of 'consistently poor' (those who combine low incomes and deprived living standards). The report then examines other features of older people's lives to see how material poverty carries over into other forms of deprivation, relating particularly to health and various forms of social integration. The findings of these analyses then provide the basis for a discussion of policy implications.

Structure of Report

The report is structured to reflect this research approach:

- Chapter 2 provides an account of the data sources and the main types of measures used.
- Chapter 3 deals with elderly incomes, taking account of certain non-cash benefits as well as cash incomes.
- Chapter 4 turns to the direct measurement of older people's living standards, focusing especially on the extent to which older people lack both basic and secondary consumption necessities.
- Chapter 5 combines the findings of Chapters 3 and 4 into a measure of the 'consistently poor' among the elderly, that is, those whose incomes are low *and* who are deprived of basic consumption necessities.
- Chapter 6 finishes off the examination of the main measures used by analysing change over time in the measures of income poverty and deprivation.
- Having described the measures of material well being used, Chapter 7 moves on to an examination of the health status of the elderly and the

relationship between income, direct deprivation and physical health. Health is a major determinant of the quality of one's life and there is a great deal of evidence that health status is itself effected by one's socio-economic position. After investigating this relationship among the elderly, this chapter then examines the usage of medical services among the elderly and whether this is effected by access to free medical services through the medical card.

- Chapter 8 extends the analysis of the health of the elderly by examining how material circumstances and physical health combine to produce particular psychological outcomes.

- Social isolation and exclusion is a particular worry among the elderly and this may be related to material circumstances, thus Chapter 9 analyses patterns of social contact among the elderly and how this varies with their economic position and other important characteristics.

- Finally, Chapter 10 brings together the findings of the previous eight chapters to get an overview of the socio-economic characteristics that contribute toward vulnerability among the elderly. Having established these, the final part of the chapter puts forward policy options and costs the different alternatives.

CHAPTER TWO

The Data

In this chapter we describe the range and structure of data used in this report. The chapter describes the rationale behind the design of the surveys used and the consequences this has for the data collected, but is not essential reading for those more interested in the substantive findings themselves. In the first section we describe the sample designs of the data sets used, whilst in the second we examine the response rates achieved at both the household and individual levels. The latter has implications for the representativeness of the data, thus the third section examines the reweighting procedures adopted for the surveys. Two of the surveys used are 'panel' surveys that often suffer from 'sample attrition' where previous respondents do not complete later interviews or are unreachable. Thus, the fourth section briefly examines the procedures used validate the representativeness of the survey data.

In an attempt to get the most up to date information possible on the material well being and quality of life of elderly people this report is mostly based upon data from the 1997 Living in Ireland Survey. However, earlier ESRI surveys are also used so that we can analyze developments in particular areas over a longer period. Data from the 1987 Survey of Income Distribution, Poverty and Usage of State Services are the earliest used, whilst from 1994 we use the first wave of the Living in Ireland Survey. All three surveys are highly comparable, but the 1994 and 1997 surveys are particularly comparable as they are the first and fourth waves respectively of the Irish component of the European Union Household Panel Survey (ECHP). As its name suggests, the ECHP is a fully harmonized survey of individuals and households carried out in 12 EU states between 1994 and 1997. The aim of the survey was to produce comparable data over time (the panel aspect) on the economic, financial and other circumstances of households throughout the E.U. The novel feature of the ECHP is its longitudinal design where the same sample of households and individuals were reinterviewed in each successive year. This allows researchers to examine the changing characteristics and socio-economic circumstances over time and thus get a clearer picture of the processes in operation. As the key aspect of the ECHP was harmonization the structure of the questionnaire, questions asked and answer codes used in participating countries were the same. However, the Irish version, 'the Living In Ireland Survey', also contained a number of modules and questions that added to the original design specified by Eurostat (the central statistical agency of the E.U.) and which allow us to examine a far wider range of subjects among the elderly population of Ireland.

Survey Sample Designs
In this section we will examine the sampling frame and design of the three surveys used. The oldest of the data sets used is the Survey of Income Distribution, Poverty and Usage of State Services carried out by the ESRI in 1987. As with the other two surveys used in this report, this was designed to provide a nationally representative sample of the population resident in private households in that year and drew its sampling frame from the Register of Electors. This has several consequences. First of all, this means that those resident in institutions such as residential or geriatric care homes will not be sampled. Similarly, migrant groups such as the traveling community or the homeless population will not be interviewed. Although these losses from the sampling frame are small (it covers 97% of the population of the state) it is still to be regretted since, as mentioned, the elderly are a group which is over represented in institutional care. It is also true that the homeless are, almost by definition far more likely to be deprived and poor than the general population. To sample populations such as these requires specific sample surveys and the general surveys used in this report are not suited to gathering information on such populations. Their omission is regrettable, but unavoidable in the circumstances.

As the sampling frame is a list of persons registered to vote, this produces a list of electors, or persons, rather than households which leads to a particular form of sample bias that we will return to shortly. The sample itself was drawn using a two stage process using the ESRI's RANSAM system which allows the District Electoral Divisions (DEDs) to be stratified according to a number of important variables (province, urban/rural location and level of unemployment) before the first stage of sampling selects a population of these DEDs. In the second stage of sampling, a systematic sample of individuals is drawn from within the selected DEDs, or groups of DEDs (depending on a minimum population threshold) to produce the target sample. In 1987, the target sample for the survey comprised 5,850 households selected as 225 clusters of 26 households (electors) each. In 1994, the target sample was 259 clusters or DEDs each with 28 households yielding 7,252 households in total. As the 1997 survey was the fourth wave of the same panel as 1994 it reinterviewed all individuals where possible from the households contacted in 1994 (and subsequently interviewed in 1995 and 96).

Sample Size Attained
In 1987, of the total sample selected of 5,850 households, 615 could not be contacted and 70 more turned out to be institutions or organizations. Of the

remaining households (or 'effective sample'), 3,321 households or 64.3% responded to the survey (9.4% could not subsequently be contacted and 2.2% were too ill to be interviewed). Of the responding households a further 14 were excluded because of missing information (notably on income) leaving a sample for analysis of 3,310 households (64.1% of the effective sample and 56.6% of the original selection). These household interviews translated into 6,784 personal interviews with household members on a number of different subjects.

In 1994, of the 7,252 households originally selected for the sample, 166 were institutions or were ineligible for interview leaving an effective sample of 7,086 households. Of these households, contact could not be established with 609 households leaving 6,477 valid addresses that were contacted and 4,048 where actual interviews took place (28.2% refused). This meant that 57.1% of the effective sample were interviewed and 62.5% of the valid contacted addresses. A total of 14,583 persons were members of these 4,048 households, 10,411 of which were eligible for interview and 9,905 of whom completed the full interview questionnaire (964 on a proxy basis). The 506 eligible people who did not respond represent less than 5% of eligible persons in responding households.

Reweighting of Data

There are a number of different sources of bias that can effect the results of social surveys that are usually dealt with by reweighting the data. First of all, samples can be adversely effected by differential non-response among the original sample selected. As the last section showed, both the 1987 and 1994 surveys failed to interview all those selected from the original sampling frame. If some groups, or people/households with particular characteristics are more prone to non-response than others this can lead to bias in the results if not dealt with. However, bias can also be introduced by the design of the survey. As already mentioned, all the surveys used in this report are sampled from a survey frame of those registered to vote which is the population of voters in private households and thus people rather than households. Leaving aside the absence of travelers, households headed by under 18s or the institutionalized, this design has the characteristic that it over represents larger households since these will, on average contain more people eligible to vote.

'Reweighting' entails creating a value for each case that either increases or decreases its impact on the sample as a whole. Thus, if there are a larger proportion of say, men rather than women in the sample than other statistical sources such as the census suggest that there should be, these can be given a weight that reflects their 'true' prevalence. Details of the reweighting procedures are available in Appendix A.

Validating the Data

After the collection and reweighting of the data, it is important that we use other procedures to check whether the data are actually representative of the population they purport to measure using some exterior reference point or source. In the case of the Living In Ireland Survey, data from the Labour Force Survey (1994 and successive years), 1991 Census of the Population and administrative statistics from the Department of Social Welfare were used for comparison.

Looking first at the representativeness of the Living in Ireland surveys in terms of basic demographic distributions, comparisons to the 1991 Census and subsequent Labour Force Surveys (LFS) showed that the age/sex distributions were extremely close with the largest sub-group variation being less than 1%. Further comparisons to the LFS showed that the distribution of households with varying numbers in work and unemployment were very acceptable.

However, some differences did appear in comparisons between published information from the Department of Social Welfare on the numbers receiving different types of benefits and the Living in Ireland Survey in 1994. The figures on the receipt of Unemployment Benefit/Assistance and Old Age Pensions/Retirement Pensions were very close to administrative totals (254.7 thousand compared to 256.61 in the case of types of pensions). However, the numbers stating that they received Survivors/Widows/Widower's pensions were 18 thousand persons fewer than administrative records indicated. It is difficult to definitively state why this difference occured, but the most likely reason is probably recall error on the part of respondents coupled with sample bias created through the absence of persons in institutional care from the sample. Although all care is taken at fieldwork and coding stages to eliminate ambiguity, it is difficult to exclude it completely and it may well be that those receiving Survivor's/Widow's/Widower's benefits stated that they were receiving an Old Age Contributory Pension. Some evidence for this hypothesis can be gained from adding the totals for the above pensions to those for other old age pensions which produces a grand total of 346.4 thousand compared to the administrative record of 366.32. When we take account of the 5%[1] of the potential population who are in institutional care the administrative total drops to 340 thousand, very close to the figure for the survey.

Further detail of the methodology used for the Living in Ireland Survey is available in Callan *et al* 1996.

---

[1] Department of Health Survey of Long Term Care 1997.

CHAPTER THREE

Incomes and Poverty

In this chapter, we examine the different sources and levels of income available to elderly households and characterize those elderly vulnerable to low incomes. Along with the next two chapters, this establishes a detailed picture of the material living standards of the elderly and forms the basis upon which we can go on to examine the role of other determinants of quality of life such as health and social participation. This chapter will provide an overview of the income situation of the elderly in the Living in Ireland Survey, including an examination of the level and sources of elderly incomes and how these vary by location and household type. It will also attempt to assess the role of non-cash benefits received by the elderly from the state such as subsidized electricity and gas, travel passes and free television licenses (amongst others). These benefits are received by a large proportion of the elderly and could add significantly to their material living standard by increasing disposable income.

The 1997 wave of the Living in Ireland Survey provides detailed information on the sources and levels of household and individual income that includes sources such as investments, dividends, sick pay and other regular transfers as well as employment/self-employment income and social welfare benefits. For most income sources, current income is measured as the amount received in the previous week (or the weekly equivalent of fortnightly or monthly income), although information on some sources such as self-employment income and interest and dividends covers longer periods because of their intermittent or fluctuating nature. Information on income from rent, interest and dividends was sought on amounts received in the previous twelve months and information on self-employment income was requested in the form of pre-tax profits in the most recent twelve month period for which accounts are available. Farm incomes were estimated using information from a special farm questionnaire eliciting outputs, input costs and receipts gathered (Callan et al., 1989).

All of the analyses in this chapter refer to household[1] income (i.e. the sum of individual incomes within the household). Household income is usually

---

1 Households are defined as groups of persons who live together, share some form of communal budgeting arrangement and usually meet together at least once each week for a communal meal.

conceived of as a better guide to the living standards of individuals than the income of any individual within a household alone Callan *et al.*, 1996), although this does make the assumption that household income, or at least the fruits derived from household income are shared equally amongst the members of the household according to need (Pahl, 1983; Pahl, 1989; Rottman, 1994; Nolan and Cantillon, 1998). Since we will be using a household measure of income, and as the elderly live in a diverse range of household types, it would be useful at this point to outline the household typologies to be used in this and later chapters. Given the range of circumstances within which the elderly live it is not possible to use a single typology, thus we will use different typologies in different circumstances. To aid comparisons over time we thought it useful to adopt the typologies used in the report by Fahey and Murray (1994), one of which was itself taken from the 1982 report by Whelan and Vaughan (1982).

The First Typology

The first typology is a three-fold classification that allows us to examine the circumstances of households with a single person compared to those with just a couple (all other households being brought together under the single category 'other'). This grouping allows us to examine whether single elderly people are in a more vulnerable position to elderly people living in a couple.

The Second Typology

The second typology is more complex, but allows us to look at the position of various categories of elderly households compared to different categories of non-elderly households. This classification covers all private households and centers on the age of the 'head of household' and whether there are elderly or children present. The household head was nominated by the household as the owner or tenant of the accommodation, or the eldest of two or more people deemed responsible for the accommodation:

- Family with children under 16 and no elderly;
- household with head of household aged 65 to 74;
- household with a head of household aged 75 plus;
- household headed by an under 65, but with elderly;
- household without children under 16 or elderly.

The Third Typology

The third typology uses the differentiation between children (under 14s), adults (14 to 64) and the elderly (65 or over) to produce a typology that is useful for when comparing types of elderly households (and thus only covers households containing an elderly person), but to a more detailed level than that used in the first typology. The categories are:

- Elderly person alone;
- 2 or more elderly people;
- 1 or more elderly, 1 adult, no children;
- 1 or more elderly, 2 adults, no children;
- 1 or more elderly, 1 or more adults, with children.

If we cross-classify the second and third household types (see table 3.1), it is clear that the vast majority of elderly people live in households headed by an elderly person (91.7%). Interestingly, if elderly are present in households containing adults, but no children, the elderly are more often the head of household (over 78%), whereas if children are present, the under 65 is more likely to be the head of household (elderly person in 43% of cases).

Table 3.1: Cross-tabulation of Household Types Two and Three

Household Composition	Household with Head Aged 65-74	Household with Head Aged 75 or Over	Household Headed by an Under 65 with Elderly	Total
Elderly Person Alone	22.1	21.7	-	43.8
Two or More Elderly People	10.8	11.3	-	22.1
1 or More Elderly, 1 Adult, No Children	9.1	5.1	3.1	17.3
1 or More Elderly, 2 or More Adults, No Children	8.5	1.4	2.7	12.6
1 or More Elderly, 1 or More Adults, With Children	1.5	0.3	2.4	4.2
Total	52.0	39.7	8.3	100

Elderly Incomes by Source

Now that we have established some typologies within which to analyze the incomes of elderly households we can turn to an examination of the main sources of this income. Figure 3.1 shows the composition of elderly household incomes by household type (the third of those mentioned above). Among those households in figure 3.1 containing just elderly people, by far the largest part of household income is provided by occupational or social welfare pensions. Reliance on social welfare pensions is greatest among elderly people living alone. On average, social welfare pensions make up 70% of their total income, a

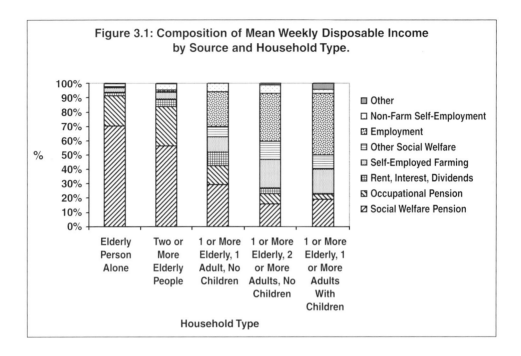

Figure 3.1: Composition of Mean Weekly Disposable Income by Source and Household Type.

figure that rises to over 90% if we include occupational pensions. In households with more than one elderly person the proportion of income derived from pensions falls to 84%, but is still by far the largest source.

As we move from left to right in figure 3.1, the household types begin to be more mixed in terms of elderly and non-elderly people and as we would expect this leads to a greater proportion of income being derived from employment, farming and other types of social welfare. Interestingly, although income from interest and dividends is often taken to be a major component of incomes amongst the elderly, on average it only makes up 2.5% of the total incomes of elderly people living alone and 5% of two or more elderly living together.

What types of pension contribute most to these totals? Table 3.2 shows the mean contribution of different pension sources to the mean totals observed in figure 3.1. Among the elderly living alone, old age contributory pensions and widow's contributory pensions each make up a quarter of total income, followed closely by occupational pensions which together form 20% and non-contributory old age pensions which form 16%. The large proportion provided by widow's pensions is indicative of the make up of the single elderly group which is 70% female[2]. If we look at households containing two or more elderly, old age contributory and

---

[2] 93% of recipients of Widow(ers) Pensions are female (Statistical Report on Social Welfare 1997).

Table 3.2: Composition of Weekly Income of Households Containing Elderly Persons By Household Type and Proportion of Income from Each Source

			Type of Household			
Source of Income	Elderly Person Alone	Two or More Elderly People	1 or More Elderly, 1 Adult, No Children	1 or More Elderly, 2 or More Adults No Children	1 or More Elderly, 1 or More Adults with Children	All Households
Social Welfare Retirement Pension	£1.53 (1.5%)	£1.30 (0.7%)	£5.30 (2.0%)	£3.89 (0.86%)	£1.60 (0.4%)	£0.64 (0.2%)
Old Age Contributory Pension	£24.95 (24.7%)	£71.97 (36%)	£33.42 (12.8%)	£34.27 (7.6%)	£24.73 (6.7%)	£10.03 (3.1%)
Old Age Non-Contributory Pension	£16.10 (16%)	£37.14 (18.6%)	£20.06 (7.7%)	£22.06 (4.9%)	£11.96 (3.2%)	£5.79 (1.8%)
Pre-Retirement Allowance	£0.11 (0.1%)	£0 (0%)	£0.30 (0.1%)	£1.98 (0.4%)	£0 (0%)	£1.04 (0.3%)
Widows Contributory Pension	£24.92 (24.7%)	£2.59 (1.3%)	£12.54 (4.8%)	£5.14 (1.1%)	£29.86 (8.1%)	£6.49 (2.0%)
Widows Non-Contributory Pension	£3.29 (3.3%)	£0.41 (1.3%)	£4.79 (1.8%)	£4.09 (0.91%)	£2.79 (0.8%)	£1.09 (0.3%)
Public Sector Occupational Pension	£11.94 (11.8%)	£21.65 (10.8%)	£14.20 (5.5%)	£16.96 (3.8%)	£6.56 (1.8%)	£5.93 (1.8%)
Private Sector Occupational Pension	£9.20 (9.1%)	£32.95 (16.5%)	£19.40 (7.4%)	£16.01 (3.6%)	£5.92 (1.6%)	£8.09 (2.5%)
Other	£8.80 (8.7%)	£32.08 (16%)	£148.75 (57%)	£344.04 (76.2%)	£284.74 (76.9%)	£289.47 (88.1%)
Total Income	£100.84 (100%)	£200.09 (100%)	£260.76 (100%)	£451.44 (100%)	£370.16 (100%)	£328.57 (100%)

Table 3.3: Receipt and Reliance on Types of Income by Elderly Household Type (Reliance=66% or More of Total Income)

Income Source	Elderly Person Alone		Two or More Elderly People		All Types Containing Persons Aged Over 64	
	% Households Receiving Income Type	%Receiving 'Reliant' on Income Type	% Households Receiving Income Type	%Receiving 'Reliant' on Income Type	% Households Receiving Income Type	%Receiving 'Reliant' on Income Type
Employment	0.2	0	2.1	7.6	16.5	18.1
Non-Farm Self-Employment	0.8	26.1	2.3	10.7	2.3	29.4
Self-Employed Farm	3.1	39.0	11.0	7.7	13.2	15.8
Occupational Pension	30.3	14.6	44.1	30.5	32.2	17.9
Social Welfare Pension	94.1	81.9	89.4	74.2	88.8	61.7
Interest/Dividends	25.7	3.1	40.3	1.7	33.8	2.3
Other Social Welfare Income	1.5	21.0	0.3	0	12.4	2.4

non-contributory pensions come to predominate followed by private and public sector occupational pensions which together make up over 27% of the total income of these types of households. Once again, if we move from left to right in table 3.2, other forms of income become more important as the household type comes to include more working age adults and then children.

However, these 'mean' income contributions are averages across the elderly population and do not tell us a great deal about the role of particular types of income for those actually receiving that source of income. Table 3.3 shows the proportion of two types of elderly households receiving particular types of income and what proportion of those who receive are reliant upon this source. Reliance here is defined as making up two thirds or more of household income. Table 3.3 confirms the role of social welfare pensions in the finances of elderly households. It shows that the vast majority of single and dual person elderly households receive these sources and that they make up three-quarters or more of household income. Occupational pensions also contribute substantially to elderly households' incomes, though more in two or more person households than amongst the single elderly. It is useful to note that although self-employment and farming income are received by a very small minority of pensioners, they make up a sizable proportion of these single elderly households' incomes. On the other hand, and as remarked upon above, although income from interest and dividends are received by one in four of single and two fifths of dual elderly households, very few rely on these types of incomes. Table 3.3a shows similar information, but this time for social welfare benefits alone.

The Level and Distribution of Elderly Incomes
Having established the main components of elderly incomes, we can now go on to look at their level and distribution and compare those of the elderly to the Irish population in general. We can also begin to look at how other personal and household characteristics effect income and begin to get a better grip on those characteristics that make some elderly more vulnerable to low standards of living than others. At this point however, we also need to consider the problem of 'equivalence'. When we compare the income of one household to another and draw conclusions about its adequacy, we have to be careful that we are comparing like with like in terms of the number of people living off the amount in the household. A small income may be adequate for a household with few members, but will not be for a larger number of people. To control for this we apply 'equivalence scales' to household income to reflect the number of people covered.

There are three different equivalence scales that have been used in the Irish context, each of which makes slightly different assumptions about the 'weight' that should be attached to the presence of additional adults (aged 15 plus) and

Table 3.3a: Receipt and Reliance on Types of Income by Elderly Household Type (Reliance=66% or More of Total Income)

Income Source	Elderly Person Alone		Two or More Elderly People		All Types Containing Persons Aged Over 64	
	% Households Receiving Income Type	%Receiving 'Reliant' on Income Type	% Households Receiving Income Type	%Receiving 'Reliant' on Income Type	% Households Receiving Income Type	%Receiving 'Reliant' on Income Type
Social Welfare Retirement Pension	1.9	100	1.9	0	2.6	43.3
Old Age Contributory Pension	31.2	82.8	64.8	41.4	39.8	46.7
Old Age Non-Contributory Pension	23.5	84.7	43.9	34.5	27.8	45.2
Pre-Retirement Allowance	0.2	100	-	0	0.5	24.5
Widows Contributory Pension	32.5	75.8	3.6	13.8	20.7	54.9
Widows Non-Contributory Pension	4.8	96.6	0.5	100	4.4	49.7
Public Sector Occupational Pension	14.6	16.5	19.9	22.4	15.5	16.5
Private Sector Occupational Pension	16.8	12.0	25.3	31.5	17.6	15.9
Other Social Welfare	0	0	0	0	0.1	0

any children (aged up to 14) after the first person is given a weight of 1:

- Scale A: 0.66 for additional adults and 0.33 for children. This scale is close to the implicit scale in the rates of unemployment assistance in Ireland when child benefits are also taken into account.
- Scale B: 0.6 for additional adults and 0.4 for children. This is close to the scale implicit in the rates of income support in the UK.
- Scale C: 0.7 for additional adults and 0.5 for children. This is the old scale adopted by the OECD for international comparisons that has recently been replaced with a new scale based on the weightings of 0.5 and 0.3.

Table 3.4 shows the proportions of elderly households falling into different income bands for unequivalised incomes and for each of the equivalence scales. As we would expect given the results in table 3.2, almost 70% of elderly households have unequivalised incomes of £200 or less a week and over one third live on £100 or less. Table 3.4 shows that applying the equivalence scales has the effect of moving an even larger proportion of elderly households into the bottom three income bands such that 90% of elderly households have an income of £200 or less per 'equivalised individual' per week on all scales. There is some evidence in table 3.4 that scales that place a higher weight on each additional individual have a greater tendency to compress a greater proportion of elderly households into the lowest two income bands, but the effect is not significant (P=0.7). To simplify presenta-

Table 3.4: Proportion in Different Household Net Income Bands Amongst Elderly: Unequivalised and Equivalised by Household Size Using Different Scales

Weekly disposable Income Band	Unequivalised	Scale A (.66 & .33)	Scale B (.6 & .4)	Scale C (.7 & .5)
Less than £50	1.5	3.9	3.8	4.2
£51-£100	34.0	55.6	55.0	56.5
£101-£200	33.9	31.0	31.0	30.3
£201-£300	11.7	6.4	7.0	6.0
£301-£400	7.9	2.1	2.4	2.1
£401-£500	4.0	0.2	-	0.2
£501-£600	1.9	0.1	0.3	0.1
Over £600	5.1	0.6	0.6	0.6
Total	100	100	100	100

Table 3.5: Proportion in Different Equivalised Household Net Income Bands Amongst Elderly by Type of Household and Area Using Equivalence Scale A (.66 & .33)

Weekly Disposable Income Band	Urban areas				Rural Areas				All Areas			
	Single Person	Couple	Other	All	Single Person	Couple	Other	All	Single Person	Couple	Other	All
Less than £50	0.7	5.2	5.5	3.1	4.5	4.1	5.6	4.9	2.3	4.7	5.6	3.9
£51-£100	64.6	42.2	45.6	53.7	82.5	67.9	28.6	57.9	72.2	52.6	36.2	55.6
£101-£200	29.8	35.3	31.4	31.6	10.1	17.9	56.7	30.4	21.4	28.3	45.4	31.0
£201-£300	3.3	13.2	12.0	8.2	2.5	6.4	5.2	4.4	3.0	10.5	8.3	6.4
£301-£400	1.4	1.6	3.6	2.1	.4	3.1	3.4	2.1	1.0	2.2	3.5	2.1
£401-£500	-	1.2	-	0.3	-	-	-	-	-	0.7	-	0.2
£501-£600	-	-	0.4	0.1	-	0.7	-	0.1	-	0.3	0.2	0.1
Over £600	0.4	1.4	1.4	0.9	-	-	0.5	0.2	0.2	0.8	0.9	0.6
Total	100	100	100	100	100	100	100	100	100	100	100	100

tion, only equivalence scale A will be used throughout the rest of this chapter. As already stated, this scale is closest to the relativities implicit in the Irish social welfare system and sensitivity tests show that the broad pattern of results is not affected by use of scale A as opposed to B or C.

Using equivalence scale A, we can begin to analyze the distribution of incomes by other characteristics. Table 3.5 shows the proportions of elderly households falling into different income bands by the first household type introduced earlier on and the geographical area of the household categorized into a rural/urban dichotomy. Bearing in mind that we are looking at the income per equivalised individual in the household, the last four columns on the right of table 3.5 show that elderly people living alone are in a worse position compared to other types of elderly households. Almost three-quarters of single elderly households live on £100 or less per week compared to 57% of couple households and 42% of 'other' types.

These inequalities by household type are matched by differences by geographical area with those in rural locations being far more likely to be in the lower end of the income distribution. For instance, although almost two-thirds of single elderly households in urban areas live on £100 or less per week, the figure is almost nine-tenths in rural locations. Similarly, amongst two person households in urban areas almost half live on £100 or less, but almost three-quarters do so in rural areas.

Comparing Elderly and Non-Elderly Households
The previous sections have shown that elderly households are reliant on a small range of different types of pension income. Because of this, the spread, or variation in elderly household incomes is extremely limited such that 90% of elderly households live on £200 or under a week per equivalised person, and 60% on £100 or less. How do elderly incomes compare to those of the Irish population in general?

Table 3.6 shows the results of a cross-classification between household type and equivalised income categories that order the population in the 1997 Living in Ireland Survey into ten equal groups or 'deciles' with those with the highest incomes in the 'top' decile and those with the lowest in the 'bottom'. By examining what proportion of each household type falls into each income category, we can get a better view of where the incomes of the elderly lie in comparison to the rest of the population. The household types in table 3.6 that are of most interest in this context are those in which the household head is aged 65 to 74 and 75 plus. Figure 3.2 shows the proportion of particular household types falling into the bottom 10, 20, 30 and 40% of the income distribution. It shows that elderly households are under represented in the very bottom decile, but over represented in the bottom half of the income distribution overall. The relatively narrow income band into which most of the elderly are concentrated is

Table 3.6: Equivalised Disposable Household Income (.66 & .33) Decile By Household Type

Equivalised Household Disposable Income Decile	Households without Elderly, with Children	Households without Elderly or Children	Household Head 65-74	Households Head >74	Households Head <65 & 1+ Elderly	All Types
Bottom	13.8	10.0	4.5	4.3	7.3	10
2	4.6	5.2	24.9	26.6	4.9	10
3	6.7	6.4	16.5	26.3	11.4	10
4	9.7	7.9	12.5	15.1	8.2	10
5	12.5	6.6	8.2	11.2	23.6	10
6	14.9	7.7	8.4	3.3	7.5	10
7	12.2	10.0	7.1	4.8	13.8	10
8	11.2	10.8	9.6	3.7	3.4	10
9	8.5	16.3	4.2	2.7	6.7	10
Top	6.1	19.2	3.9	2.0	13.0	10
Total	100	100	100	100	100	100

Type of Household

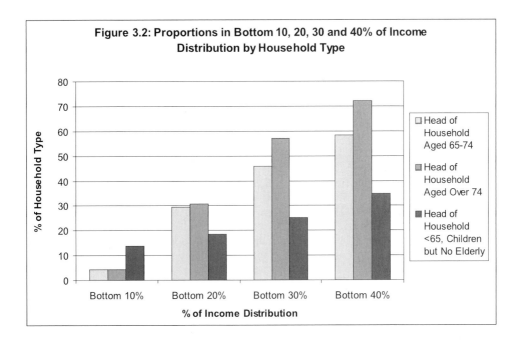

Figure 3.2: Proportions in Bottom 10, 20, 30 and 40% of Income Distribution by Household Type

high enough to keep the majority of elderly households above the lowest reaches of the national income distribution, but too low to bring them up to the national average.

In fact, large proportions of the elderly are found in the second and third income deciles, that is just above the very lowest category, but quite a distance still from the middle of the national income distribution. Households with a head aged over 74 are particularly concentrated between the bottom 20 and 40% of the income distribution with three-fifths of this type appearing in the bottom 30%.

Different types of elderly households show differing risks of being at the bottom of the income distribution. Table 3.7 uses a more detailed typology of elderly households and shows that elderly people living on their own are much more likely than other elderly, or households with non-elderly to be found in the bottom 30% of the distribution and 2.5 times more likely than households with no elderly.

In summary then, the evidence presented so far shows that elderly households are reliant on a small range of different types of pension income and that there is relatively little variation among the elderly in terms of income level. However, elderly households tend to be near the bottom of the national income distribution, although levels of pension income provide a basic safety net that prevents large proportions of the elderly falling into the lowest income category.

Table 3.7 Equivalised Disposable Household Income (.66 & .33) Decile By Elderly Household Type

Equivalised Household Disposable Income Decile	Elderly Person Alone	Two or More Elderly People	1 or More Elderly, 1 Adult, No Children	1 or More Elderly, 2 or More Adults, No Children	1 or More Elderly, 2 or More Adults, With Children	No Elderly	All Types
Bottom	3.8	8.1	7.8	7.6	14.0	11.3	10
2	25.2	2.9	12.3	9.9	5.4	8.1	10
3	36.9	15.3	13.1	2.9	6.7	5.6	10
4	8.7	33.4	13.6	10.4	13.9	8.1	10
5	9.8	12.9	13.2	14.1	24.1	9.1	10
6	2.2	8.9	9.0	12.8	24.0	11.0	10
7	3.9	5.1	13.7	19.2	5.3	10.9	10
8	5.9	6.3	5.4	11.3	1.0	11.2	10
9	2.4	4.4	6.9	3.1	1.0	12.2	10
Top	1.2	2.7	5.0	8.5	4.5	12.5	10
Total	100	100	100	100	100	100	100

Amongst the elderly, those living alone tend to have lower incomes even after equivalisation for household size, especially those in rural locations.

Elderly Households and Income Poverty
We have seen that elderly households are more likely to appear at the bottom of the income distribution, but does this mean that their incomes are such that they are in poverty? Of course the answer to this question depends a great deal upon how we define 'poverty'. The conceptualization and measurement of poverty is a much debated area, but rather than reiterate arguments made elsewhere (Piachaud, 1987; Townsend, 1979; Callan *et al.*, 1996; Nolan and Whelan, 1996) we can side step these questions if we adopt the approach taken in the National Anti-Poverty Strategy Report (NAPS 1997) which has come to be seen as the poverty benchmark in the Irish context.

The NAPS report adopts an explicitly relative definition of poverty and combines two different types of poverty measure to produce a single poverty threshold. One measure is based purely upon the disposable income level of the household, but this is combined with a second based upon the absence of particular 'necessities' from a household through lack of resources (rather than by choice). The next chapter will discuss this second measure in more detail and outline the results amongst the elderly of applying this and chapter five will examine the combined measure of poverty as used in the NAPS report. In this chapter, on the other hand, we will concentrate on the first, that of relative disposable income, to see to what extent the elderly can be said to be in poverty by this measure.

Table 3.8 shows the risk of income poverty at the 40, 50 and 60% poverty thresholds for elderly and non-elderly households using equivalence scale 'A'. At

Table 3.8: Equivalised Risk of Poverty By Household Type (Scale A)

Household Composition	*Percentage Below Threshold*		
	40%	*50%*	*60%*
Non-elderly Households with Children	10.7	22.9	33.0
Non-elderly Households Without Children	6.0	16.4	25.8
Household Head 65-74	5.6	30.9	54.7
Household Head >74	3.9	27.4	66.0
HOH <65 & 1+ Elderly	8.5	15.6	29.3
Total	7.6	21.9	36.4

the 40% level, elderly-headed households have the lowest levels of poverty, whereas they have the highest at 50%. At the 50% level, households with a head over 74 are 25% more likely than average to be in poverty and those where the head is 65 to 74, over 40% more likely. At the 60%, this gap increases with the two groups being 81% and 50% respectively more likely to be in poverty.

Therefore, although the elderly seemed to be protected from poverty at the 40% level, the limited variation in their incomes means that over a quarter fall under the 50% and over half below the 60% poverty lines.

Non-Cash Benefits, Poverty and the Elderly
Although the above analyses tend to suggest that there is a high level of poverty amongst the elderly at the 50 and 60% mean income levels, this does not take any account of the contribution that non-cash benefits may make to the disposable incomes of the elderly. 'Free' benefits in kind, or non-cash benefits may make a substantial contribution to the living standards of the elderly and those in the households of the elderly. Free travel, electricity and television licenses were introduced in 1967-8, but this list has been added to more recently by the availability of free gas and solid fuel and subsidized telephone rental. The period from 1987 was one of particular growth in the take up of these benefits due to the awareness campaigns of pressure groups for the elderly and other possible beneficiaries. As shown in figure 3.3, the number of those receiving non-cash benefits increased strongly and by almost 100,000 in the case of

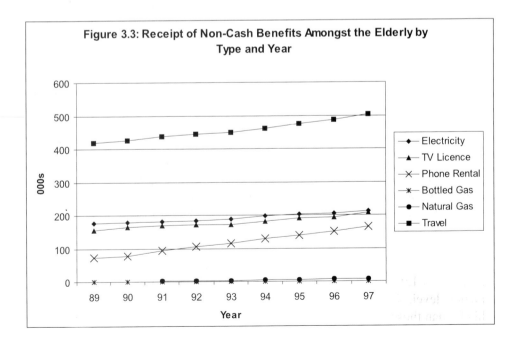

Figure 3.3: Receipt of Non-Cash Benefits Amongst the Elderly by Type and Year

telephone rental, a figure far higher than the increase in the number aged over 65. As we will go on to see in Chapter 7, 70% of those aged over 65 also have a medical card, or are covered by another member of their household's card, which entitles them to free medical treatment.

If a single elderly household were to receive all of these, except the medical card benefits weekly, they would be worth £13.69 at 1997 prices which is roughly 13% of the mean income for this type of household. Forthcoming work by the ESRI has estimated that access to a medical card can add approximately £8.70 per week to this total simply in terms of the costs of visits to a general practitioner for elderly people (and pharmacy). As we will go on to see in chapter 7, older people tend to have a greater need for health care services than younger age groups. Together and at maximum value, these benefits mean that a single elderly person would receive over a fifth extra income. Unfortunately non-cash benefits are not equivalent to cash income and it is not a simple matter to include them in our poverty calculations (Callan et al., 1989; Moffit, 1989) especially in the case of the medical card. Since we cannot be sure whether any of the elderly households would have paid for any of these services if they were not provided for free or were subsidized, we are almost certainly over-estimating their value to recipients if we simply impute a cash value. Aside from the behavioural assumptions, estimation of the value of the medical card is also complicated by the fact that the cost of services and treatment varies a great deal. Similarly, it is not clear what use free services such as a bus pass would be in a rural area with very little public transport provision. Methodological problems aside for the moment, there is also an issue here of whether non-cash benefits, particularly those such as the bus pass should be seen as a social right among the elderly, rather than as a state transfer to those on low incomes. The inclusion of the medical card as well as 'direct' lifestyle benefits also raises the question of whether we should take other forms of subsidy, say of the costs of private tertiary education through the tax payer into account in assessing income (as is standard practice in the national accounts).

Given these caveats, it seems more acceptable to estimate the role of direct benefits such as electricity and travel, rather than the more conceptually and empirically complicated medical card into account. However, in interpreting the findings we should bear this decision in mind. On this basis, what difference would the inclusion of 'direct' non-cash benefits have made on levels of poverty amongst the elderly?

Figure 3.4 shows the level of take up of non-cash benefits amongst those over 64 in the 1997 Living in Ireland Survey by whether in poverty at the 50% mean income level. Figure 3.4 clearly shows that those in income poverty are more likely than those who are not to receive all these non-cash benefits, although in

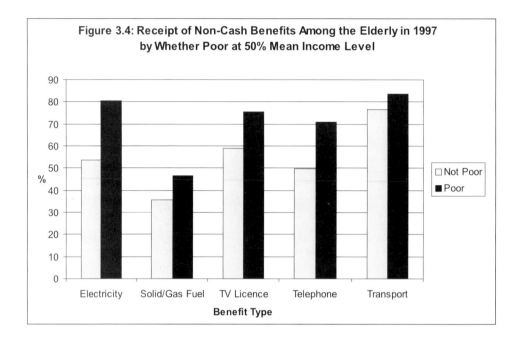

Figure 3.4: Receipt of Non-Cash Benefits Among the Elderly in 1997 by Whether Poor at 50% Mean Income Level

the case of some such as the free bus pass, or TV license, the gap between the groups is relatively small. Receipt of all these five benefits is high; even among those who are not in poverty receipt of a bus pass runs at almost 80% and around half have subsidized telephones.

Analyses of the take up of non-cash benefits by location also show a clear difference in rates between urban and rural dwellers across all types. For instance, 41% of urban elderly households compared to 37% of rural households receive a fuel allowance, 67% compared to 61% a free TV licence and 59% compared to 53% subsidized phone use (all differences are significant). Such findings should confirm our scepticism about the accuracy of the statistics to come on the effect of non-cash benefits on income poverty rates as the behavioural assumptions underlying their construction clearly do not hold.

Having made clear the assumptions and taking due note of warnings about the accuracy of our calculations of the incomes of the elderly when including non-cash benefits, we can tentatively examine the effect of receipt on the proportions in poverty at the 50% level in 1997 in figure 3.5. Adding in an imputed value for non-cash benefits has a dramatic effect on the levels of income poverty at the 50% level. When adjusted, the added income means that the proportions in poverty in the elderly categories are lower than in those with no elderly present. However, if we look at the effect on the proportions under the 60% income poverty line in figure 3.6 we see very little change in the relative position of different household types, although there is a decrease in the proportions of both

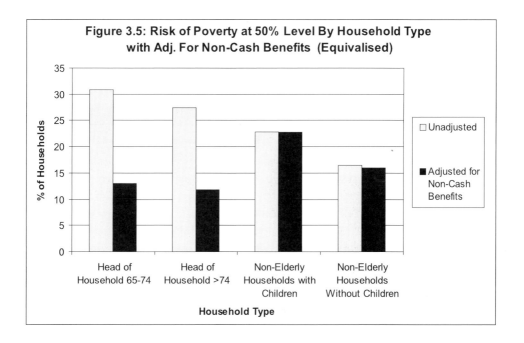

Figure 3.5: Risk of Poverty at 50% Level By Household Type with Adj. For Non-Cash Benefits (Equivalised)

types of elderly households in poverty. These results suggest that non-cash benefits may have a significant effect on the rates of income poverty at the 50% level, but that it is unlikely that their value would be large enough to lift the majority above the 60% line. Just to reiterate the earlier warning, the methods

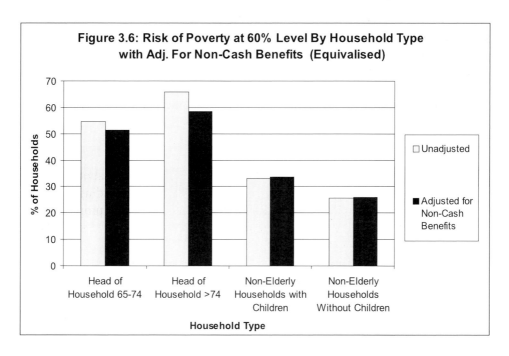

Figure 3.6: Risk of Poverty at 60% Level By Household Type with Adj. For Non-Cash Benefits (Equivalised)

used here make very generous assumptions and even then the difference at the 60% income poverty line are minimal.

Wealth and Assets

So far in this chapter we have confined ourselves to the current income of households and its implications for present living standards. This has shown that elderly incomes tend to fall within a narrow range in the lower part of the income distribution. However, current income takes no account of the degree of savings, wealth and assets among elderly households unless those assets produce a regular income, or a dividend in the year before the survey. Yet past research has shown that the retired have the highest levels of financial assets in terms of deposits, savings and sophisticed financial instruments (Honohan & Nolan, 1993; Whelan and Vaughan 1982) and that those over 64 also have a greater probability of being home owners. There is evidence to support this earlier research in the 1997 Living in Ireland Survey. Table 3.9 shows the mean and median value of stocks/shares and savings held by households where the head is aged over or under 65. In the case of both stocks/shares and savings, 'elderly' households have significantly higher mean assets than households headed by a person aged under 65. The zero median for the value of stocks and shares betrays the overwhelming majority of households which do not have these assets (76% of non-elderly households and 86% of elderly).

A far smaller proportion of elderly and non-elderly households have no savings, but as with stocks and shares, the elderly are more likely than non-elderly to be without (24% compared to 30%). Where the elderly do have savings, they tend to have a higher amount.

How much variation is there in the holding and value of these assets among the elderly and do these patterns match those we have already seen in current income?

Table 3.10 shows that there is a large variation in whether households actually have stocks/shares and savings by household type with the single elderly and multiple generation households being the least likely to have either asset. Whereas

Table 3.9: Mean and Median Value of Stocks/Shares and Savings by Whether Head of Household is Aged Over 65

Household Type	Value Stocks/Shares			Value Savings		
	Mean	St. Dev	Median	Mean	St. Dev	Median
Non-Elderly	1566.48	7153.72	0	4115.92	8781.15	875
Elderly	1581.84	10525.5	0	5325.34	11863	1250
All Households	1570.01	8055.4	0	4394.2	9592	900

Table 3.10: Proportions with Stocks/Shares and Savings by Household Type Containing Elderly

Household Type	% With Stocks/Shares	% With Savings
Elderly Person Alone	11.6	65.5
Elderly Couple	12.5	76.6
1+ Elderly, 1 Adult, No Children	24.9	71.9
1+ Elderly, 2+ Adults, No Children	19.1	77.7
1+ Elderly, 2+ Adults, with Children	9.9	65.9
All Households Containing Elderly	15.0	70.6

only 12% of the single elderly have stocks and shares, this figure rises to almost 25% among households containing an elderly person with a non-elderly person. When interpreting this finding, it is useful to bear in mind that the majority of these households will be couples with an older husband who is over 65. Thus, this group could be seen as younger 'elderly couples'. The second last row of table 3.10 once again shows the difficulties that multiple generation households experience, although it must be remembered that this is rather a small group and we should not attach too much weight to this finding statistically.

Table 3.11 shows the means and standard deviations for the value of these assets by the same elderly household typology and restates the large variation in holdings between different household types.

Table 3.11: Mean Value of Stocks/Shares and Savings by Household Type Containing Elderly

Household Type	Value Stocks/Shares		Value Savings	
	Mean	St. Dev	Mean	St. Dev
Elderly Person Alone	425.8	3128.3	3682.7	8497.8
Elderly Couple	1416.1	6929.5	6883.6	15696.6
1+ Elderly, 1 Adult, No Children	3387.5	15258.8	8623.5	13631.2
1+ Elderly, 2+ Adults, No Children	4385.1	19821.7	5782.5	11602.1
1+ Elderly, 2+ Adults, with Children	331.6	1524.9	3163.4	7380.5
All Households Containing Elderly	1651.7	10341.9	5487.9	11884.7

Savings and stocks and shares are not the only forms of assets held by elderly people however. Currently and historically, Ireland has always had a high rate of home ownership, thus a large proportion of elderly Irish people are home owners, the vast majority of whom have little or no outstanding debt on their property (Honohan & Nolan, 1993, p46). In fact, measured as the market value of the house less any outstanding mortgage debt, wealth in the form of housing has been estimated by Honohan and Nolan (1993, p47) to make up 55% of the total wealth of all households. Moreover, this proportion grows quickly the lower the current income of the household (and the lower the value of savings and other assets). One of the recommendations of the 1988 report of the Working Party on Services for the Elderly (The Years Ahead – A Policy for the Elderly) was that government should work with financial institutions to encourage elderly people to make use of the equity they have in residential properties to improve their standard of living. Given this, we will briefly examine the extent of home ownership among the elderly in the 1997 Living in Ireland Survey and the possibilities that this holds for different types of elderly households.

Table 3.12 shows well the high level of home ownership in Ireland. Around 75% of households own or are buying their homes and this rises to almost 81% among the elderly. Furthermore, whereas only 36% of owner-occupier households where the head is aged under 65 own their property outright, this rises to 92% among those with a head aged over 65. As with the distribution of assets and savings however, home ownership is unevenly distributed among elderly households. Whereas 85% of elderly couples own their own home, this is true of only 75% of the single elderly. There is also an interesting pattern of home ownership associated with the income poverty lines used earlier in this chapter.

Table 3.12: Housing Tenure by Age of Head of Household (%)

Housing Tenure	Age of Head of Household		
	Less than 65	Over 65	All
Owner	72.7	80.6	74.5
Local Authority Tenant	4.9	5.9	5.1
Rent Free	1.7	3.6	2.1
Private Sector Tenant	20.8	10.0	18.3
Total	100	100	100

Although at the 50% line there is very little difference in the proportion of elderly people owning their own homes, the 60% line proves to be a more useful division. Whereas table 3.12 shows that almost 81% of elderly households own their homes, this is true of only 72% of those with current incomes below the 60% line. Above the line, the proportion rises to almost 93%. This large difference suggests that those above the 60% line are far more likely to have had high incomes before retirement and have significant current resources. Some evidence in support of this comes in the form of the average value of the homes of those households headed by an elderly person above the 60% line. The houses of those above the line are worth 19% more than the average 'elderly' household and 43% more than those under the line. Similarly, if we return to possession of stocks/shares and savings, 26% of households above the 60% line have stocks/shares compared to 7% under the line and 86% have savings compared to 60% of those below the line.

Nonetheless, even given these large disparities between the assets of different types of elderly households, those that do own a property would be able to realize substantial sums if equity from the property were realized. Self estimates from respondents in the 1997 Survey put the average market value of homes headed by an elderly person at £58,557, a figure that rises to £74,177 for homes in urban areas.

Identifying Elderly Vulnerable to Poverty

So far we have examined the structuring of elderly incomes and have identified certain characteristics that make some elderly households more likely to have low income than others. For example, we have seen that the single elderly and those in rural areas are more likely to have lower incomes. Using tables alone, it is difficult to disentangle relationships between variables and to be sure that particular relationships are significant. Therefore, in this final section of the chapter we examine the risk of experiencing relative income poverty in a multi-variate statistical framework.

To examine these factors we use a logistic regression. The basic idea behind a logistic regression should be familiar to anyone who has ever watched horse racing. As in horse racing we want to describe the chances of something happening (winning a race, being income poor) and we express this in terms of the 'odds' of one group of people having some characteristic (which here is being in poverty), compared to another known as the reference group.

Here though, we examine the odds of different characteristics rather than different people. If the score is larger than one they face a greater risk and if less than one, a smaller risk.

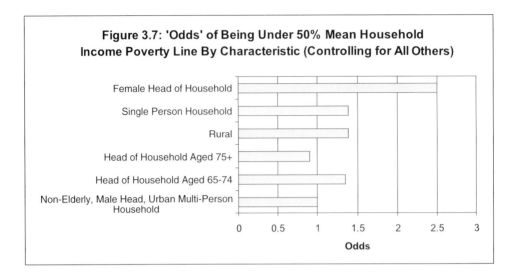

Figure 3.7: 'Odds' of Being Under 50% Mean Household Income Poverty Line By Characteristic (Controlling for All Others)

Figure 3.7 shows the results of the logistic regression on unadjusted incomes (the full model is available in Appendix B) after adding a host of household characteristics. The lowest bar in figure 3.7 represents the risk of income poverty faced by the 'reference group' of a non-elderly, male head, multi-person, urban household and each higher bar represents the effect of a particular characteristic controlling for all others.

Even after controlling for a number of variables, figure 3.7 shows that there is still a higher risk associated with having a head of household aged between 65 and 74, although the risk of those over 74 is 10% less than the reference group. However, all three of the other variables of interest are associated with higher risks of income poverty to varying degrees. Living in a rural location and living in a single person household are both almost 40% more likely to lead to income poverty whilst having a female head is 2.5 times more likely to lead to poverty. Clearly, this risk of income poverty must also be due also to the main income source of the household, thus controlling for all the variables in figure 3.7, figure 3.8 examines this variable. Once glance at figure 3.8 reveals reliance on all pension incomes other than contributory old age and occupational lead to significant and large increases in the risk of poverty. In 1997, 50% of equalivalised income averaged across households was £78.48 (using equivalence 1, .66 & .33) for a single person household. At the time of the survey, the maximum contributory pension payment was £75, a figure that increased to £80 for those over 80 with a £6 living alone allowance. Those on contributory old age pensions are not at any increased risk of poverty in the model. However, those on non-contributory pensions could receive a maximum of £64.50, or £69.50 if over 80 and they did not exceed the means test. This is £13.98 less than the poverty line leading to almost 12 times the risk of poverty. Similarly, those on

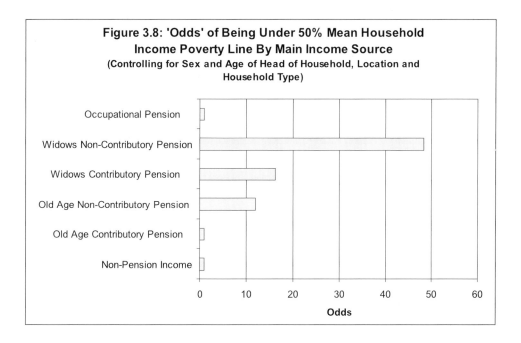

Figure 3.8: 'Odds' of Being Under 50% Mean Household Income Poverty Line By Main Income Source
(Controlling for Sex and Age of Head of Household, Location and Household Type)

contributory widow's pensions could receive £68.10 at maximum rate, and those on non-contributory pensions £64.50. Both these groups are at an increased risk of poverty (16 and 48 times the risk of those on non-pension incomes).

Now, it is legitimate to ask here whether this huge increase in risk associated with widows pensions is significant in terms of the numbers of people claiming this benefit. In terms of Widow's Contributory Pension alone, estimates from the 1997 Living In Ireland Survey show 23,802 elderly people living on this benefit were so on incomes below the 50% income poverty line and 29,960 below the 60% line. A further 25,889 elderly people relying on the Old Age Non-Contributory Pension were below the 50% income line and 44,364 below the 60% line.

Conclusions

This chapter has sought to examine the sources of income in elderly households and the level of income received, both absolutely and relative to the rest of the Irish population. The elderly are extremely reliant on social welfare pension incomes, though for some, occupational pensions also contribute a significant amount. This means first of all that the variation in incomes amongst the elderly is fairly small, but also that elderly income will be particularly sensitive to changes in the value of these sources. The limited variation in elderly incomes was made very clear in table 3.5, which showed that 90% of elderly households live on £200 or less, and almost 60% on £100 or less per 'equivalised person'.

Single elderly people are most likely amongst households containing elderly people to be found at the bottom of the income range, as are elderly people in rural locations and particularly the single elderly in rural areas.

When we compare the incomes of elderly households to the rest of the population we find that the elderly are much more likely to appear in the bottom half of the income distribution, though not at the very bottom of the income range (bottom 10%). Once again, the single elderly stand out as a group who have a high probability of being found lower in the income range.

Although elderly households are more likely to be found at the bottom of the income distribution, are they more likely to be in poverty than the general population and can we see differences in risk amongst different elderly households? This report adopts an explicitly relative line when measuring poverty and this chapter has shown that, although elderly household incomes protect the majority from falling under a poverty line set at 40% of average national household income, the elderly are more likely than other household types to be found in relative income poverty at the 50 and 60% levels. However, a majority of elderly households also receive some form of non-cash benefit that increases their disposable income and this chapter has sought to show what effect this income would have on the proportions of elderly in poverty if taken at full value. Although making clear that such analyses are tentative at best, we found that the level of non-cash benefits is sufficient to lift a large proportion of elderly households above the 50% poverty line, but not above the 60% poverty line.

Using unadjusted incomes, the final table of the chapter showed that being elderly, and particularly being an elderly female living alone in rural areas carries an increased risk of being in poverty at the 50% level. However most of this risk is accounted for by the main source of income for the household. Although those on contributory and occupational pensions are no more likely (*ceteris paribus*) than those on non-pension incomes to be under the 50% poverty line, those on non-contributory pensions and widows pensions are at a greatly increased risk.

The next chapter examines developments on a measure of standards of living based upon an index of deprivation and combines the income poverty lines with this deprivation measure to replicate the measure used in the National Ant-Poverty Strategy. Comparing all these three measures will give us a better grip on the different dimensions of the standard of living of the elderly.

CHAPTER FOUR

Levels of Life-Style Deprivation

In this chapter we augment the income analyses of the last chapter with measures that tap living patterns and customs directly by using a set of questions from the 1997 Living in Ireland Survey which ask about possession of particular items, or doing certain activities. As in the previous chapter, we will examine levels of deprivation both within the elderly population and between the elderly and the population in general. In this way we can prepare the ground for chapter 5 which compares the evidence from income and deprivation measures and combines these in a single poverty measure which is then analyzed in a longitudinal framework.

However, before we can go on to examine levels of deprivation in the elderly population, how do we go about constructing a measure of deprivation? In the first part of this chapter we will briefly describe the construction of several indexes of deprivation. Once we have established whether these indexes are coherent and valid, we can then compare levels of deprivation amongst the elderly population to the Irish population in general.

Measuring Deprivation

Drawing on work by Townsend (1979) and Mack and Lansley (1985), the 1997 Living in Ireland survey gave respondents a list of 20 items or activities and asked which were judged to be "necessities – that is things which every household (or person) should be able to have and that nobody should have to do without".

Respondents were also asked which items they actually had, or could avail of and whether lack of this item was due to lack of resources[1]. Using these questions, the first step in the analysis is to find a set of items or activities which are widely regarded as necessities by the majority of the population.

---

[1] The items included in the survey were taken from the 1987 Survey of Poverty, Income Distribution and Usage of State Services, which themselves replicated questions asked by Mack and Lansley (1985), though some changes were made to take into account Irish circumstances and items were added in 1997 to make the list more representative of current living standards

Table 4.1: Indicators of Actual Style of Living and Social Defined Necessities

Item or Activity	% Stating Necessity	% Lacking	% Experiencing Enforced Lack
A meal with meat, chicken or fish every second day if you wanted it	93.9	3.0	2.1
A warm, waterproof overcoat	97.7	4.0	2.6
Two pairs of strong shoes	95.6	5.4	4.3
A roast joint of meat or its equivalent once a week	76.4	10.8	4.2
New, not second hand clothes	86.0	7.7	6.1
Refrigerator	98.6	1.4	0.9
Washing machine	93.2	9.5	3.7
Colour TV	75.2	2.9	1.2
A dry, damp free dwelling	99.0	6.0	5.6
An indoor toilet in the dwelling which is not shared with other households	99.1	2.0	1.5
Bath or shower which is not shared with other households	99.0	3.2	2.5
Telephone	81.6	13.5	9.2
Car or Van	70.3	29.9	13.6
A weeks annual holiday away from home	62.2	44.6	32.3
Central heating in the house	80.6	17.4	10.7
To be able to save some of one's income regularly	82.4	37.6	34.8
A daily newspaper	32.8	43.4	8.9
A hobby or leisure activity	70.1	25.8	8.0
Presents for friends or family once a year	72.8	10.7	6.0
Adequate heating for your home	99.3	6.1	5.4
A second home/ A holiday home	3.1	93.6	37.6
Able to replace any worn out furniture	85.1	25.7	20.1
Having friends or family for a drink or a meal at least once a month	45.7	35.3	10.7
Home computer	14.7	78.9	22.3
Video	29.0	26.4	7.8
Microwave	30.9	38.4	11.2
Deep freeze	43.5	44.2	10.7
Dishwasher	16.0	75.1	18.8

Table 4.1 lists the responses from elderly and non-elderly households to the questions on whether an item or activity is a necessity, whether the household has the item/could avail of it and whether if they did not this was due to lack of resources.

Table 4.1 shows that items that are generally possessed also tend to be regarded as necessities and vice versa. Thus, a fridge, an indoor toilet and bath or shower are possessed by most households and are also seen as necessities, though there are some exceptions to this pattern: 85% of respondents feel that households should be able to replace worn out furniture, but over a fifth could not afford to do this.

Similarly, 82% of respondents feel that they should be able to save some of the household income regularly, but almost 35% could not do so. Nonetheless, a fairly coherent pattern emerges from the data that suggests there is a fair degree of consensus in the population about what can be regarded as necessities.

The 1997 survey also included a number of additional questions that asked about deprivation through lack of resources which are important indicators of deprivation. Unlike in the previous question sets, the format of these questions assumed that respondents lacked these items through lack of resources, though this was a safe assumption given the items. Table 4.2 lists these questions and responses.

Overall, small proportions of respondents were deprived of these items or activities through lack of resources and a particularly small proportion had gone without food or heat through lack of resources.

It would be possible at this point simply to sum those items from table 4.1 and 4.2 which respondents lack through shortage of resources giving a single scale of deprivation. This may be useful, but how do we know that deprivation is a

Table 4.2: Additional Indicators of Life-Style and Deprivation by Household Type

Item or Activity	%
Had a day in the last two weeks without a substantial meal	1.4
Had to go without heating during the last year through lack of money	1.7
Unable to afford an afternoon or evening out in the previous two weeks	7.5
Debt problems arising from ordinary living expenses	6.8

uni-dimensional concept? Could it not be that a single index may actually obscure the different effects which lack of particular items may have on lifestyle? Previous work (Callan *et al.,* 1993, 1996); (Nolan and Whelan, 1996) has identified three underlying dimensions of deprivation in the Irish context. These have been defined as a 'basic' dimension that consists of enforced lack of food and clothing, a 'housing services and durables' dimension, made up of items on housing quality and durables and a 'secondary' dimension based on lifestyle items and consumption indicators.

To check whether similar dimensions emerge from the 1997 Living in Ireland Survey data, it is necessary to see whether the items from tables 4.1 and 4.2 cluster in particular groups. The technique for doing this is is fully described in Whelan (1991) and complete results are available in Appendix C, but it is sufficient here to say that the results for 1997 are broadly similar to those of 1987 in that we get a clear distinction between all three dimensions[2].

Levels of Deprivation

Using the three deprivation scales we can now analyze levels of deprivation amongst the elderly and compare these to the Irish population in general. Tackling the latter issue first, table 4.3 compares scores on the 'basic' dimension of deprivation between households where the head is aged 65-74 or over 75 with non-elderly households with children. This table 4.3 shows that elderly households experience significantly less basic deprivation than non-elderly households with children (P=<.001). Both types of elderly household in the table have significantly higher proportions scoring zero on the deprivation scale. These findings are very interesting in view of the relatively weak income position of the elderly revealed in the last chapter.

Looking at the 'secondary' index in table 4.4, the elderly groups seem marginally more deprived than the non-elderly households (44% scoring zero compared to 50%), but this difference is actually not significant (P>0.07). In fact, a larger proportion of those aged 75 plus score three or less on this index. Thus if we use a mean score, this group are significantly less deprived than the non-elderly group. Once again then, our analysis of the secondary index shows that the elderly are in the same position, or marginally less deprived than non-elderly groups.

---

[2] To maintain consistency with previous work, the video, dishwasher, home computer, deep freeze, microwave and 'adequate heating' items from table 4.1 were not included in the factor analysis or deprivation dimensions.

Table 4.3: Distribution of Scores on Basic Deprivation Index by Household Type

	% of Type of Household			
Score	Non Elderly Household with Children	Head of Household 65-74	Head of Household >74	All Types
0	81.5	90.4	86.8	84.8
1	9.7	4.9	11.1	8.4
2	3.2	3.2	1.1	3.4
3	1.7	0.7	0.9	1.4
4	2.3	0.1	-	1.2
5	0.4	0.6	0.1	0.3
6	1.1	-	-	0.4
7 or More	0.2	-	-	0.1
Total	100	100	100	100

Table 4.4: Distribution of Scores on Secondary Deprivation Index by Household Type

	% of Type of Household			
Score	Non Elderly Household with Children	Head of Household 65-74	Head of Household >74	All Types
0	49.6	43.9	44.8	49.0
1	15.7	20.7	28.5	18.6
2	11.4	15.9	13.2	12.6
3	7.8	10.9	6.0	7.7
4	8.1	4.6	5.6	6.1
5	2.5	3.4	1.8	3.0
6	2.6	0.5	-	1.6
7 or More	2.3	0.1	-	1.3
Total	100	100	100	100

**Table 4.5: Distribution of Scores on Housing Deprivation Index
by Household Type**

| | % of Type of Household | | | |
Score	Non Elderly Household with Children	Head of Household 65-74	Head of Household >74	All Types
0	91.3	82.7	83.4	90.0
1	5.6	13.1	9.7	7.4
2	3.2	2.1	3.4	1.4
3	0.1	1.2	1.5	0.5
4	-	0.5	0.4	0.2
5	-	0.2	0.2	0.3
6	-	0.2	1.4	0.2
Total	100	100	100	100

Do we see the same result on the housing index? Table 4.5 shows that elderly households are more likely than non-elderly to lack one or more of the items on the housing index ($P<0.001$). A t-test of the means of the three household types shows that the two elderly groups have a significantly higher score than the non-elderly groups. How can we explain the different results we get from the housing index compared to the basic and secondary?

These can be explained if we reflect upon housing among the elderly. First of all, the elderly tend to have lived in their houses for longer and thus the stock of housing will be of a worse quality in this group. Second, where houses need renovation or modernization the elderly may be more 'risk averse' than younger householders and cautious about major structural changes. For instance, it may well be that the elderly are significantly more sensitive than the rest of the population to the bother and hassle involved in improving the quality of their homes. Lastly, as their houses tend to be older and in need of more work, this tends to increase the average cost of repairs to elderly homes thus making it more unlikely that they will be carried out.

We get confirmation of the evidence of a poorer quality of housing among the elderly if we examine the results for other questions in the 1997 survey that asked specifically about housing problems. Table 4.6 shows the proportions of

Table 4.6: Proportion Having Selection of Problems with Housing by Age of Head of Household

Type of Housing Problem	% Having Problem	
	Households with Head Aged <65	Households with Head Aged 65+
Lack of adequate heating	6.5	7.8
Damp walls, floors etc	7.0	11.5**
Rot in windows or floors	6.1	8.3*
Leaking roof	2.7	4.5*

Significance Key: *=<0.5 **=<0.01 ***=<.001

elderly and non-elderly households stating that they had problems with heating their homes, dampness, leaking roofs and rotting doors and windows.

Table 4.6 shows that the elderly having worse quality housing on all of these measures although they are only significantly different on three of these, having a damp home, having rotting windows and floors and leaking roofs.

Given that the elderly differ from the general population in terms of their standard of housing, are there differences in the risk of these problems between the elderly by housing tenure? Although we must be careful of the low numbers in some of the cells in table 4.7, it seems reasonably clear that those elderly in

Table 4.7: Proportion Having Selection of Problems with Housing (Head of Household Aged Over 64)

Type of Housing Problem	Housing Tenure				
	Owner	Local Auth. Housing	Rent Free	Private Sector Tenant	$\chi 2$ Sig.
Lack of adequate heating	5.9	12.5	4.0	22.1	***
Damp walls, floors etc	11.2	15.0	8.3	11.3	
Rot in windows or floors	7.1	5.0	12.0	18.3	*
Leaking roof	3.8	5.0	0.0	11.1	*
N:	552	40	25	72	

Significance Key: *=<0.5 **=<0.01 ***=<.001

private sector rented housing are significantly more likely to experience at least three of these housing problems.

Comparing Elderly Groups

Thus far we have seen that the elderly do not differ significantly from the general population on the basic and secondary deprivation indexes, but do appear to have worse quality housing on several different types of measure. We now consider variation in levels of deprivation among the elderly themselves.

Table 4.8 lists the mean scores for the basic, secondary and housing deprivation indexes for elderly households classified by household type and area. Rural households do not score significantly lower than urban households on the basic index, but are more deprived on the secondary and housing scales (both $P<0.001$). The lack of difference on the basic index is interesting since it suggests that a core standing of living is being preserved in rural households, although the significant difference on the other two scales shows the long term divergence between urban and rural populations. Rather more worrying are the indications that the housing conditions of the rural elderly are worse than the

Table 4.8: Mean Basic, Secondary and Housing Deprivation Score by Household Type and Location (Head of Household Aged Over 64)

Household Type and Location		Basic Deprivation	Secondary Deprivation	Housing Deprivation
Rural	Single Person	0.19	1.56	0.60
	Couple	0.17	1.45	0.30
	Other	0.14	1.48	0.33
	All	0.17	1.51	0.45
Urban	Single Person	0.18	0.86	0.20
	Couple	0.12	0.74	0.1
	Other	0.21	1.13	0.11
	All	0.17	0.90	0.15
All	Single Person	0.19	1.15	0.37
	Couple	0.14	1.03	0.18
	Other	0.17	1.29	0.22
	All	0.17	1.16	0.28

Table 4.9: Proportion Having Selection of Problems with Housing (Head of Household Aged Over 64)

Type of Housing Problem	Rural	Urban	All	Sig. $\chi 2$
Lack of adequate heating	9.5	6.4	7.8	-
Damp walls, floors etc	16.1	7.6	11.4	**
Rot in windows or floors	10.5	6.6	8.3	*
Leaking roof	4.9	3.9	4.4	-
N:	306	382	688	-

Significance Key: *=<0.5 **=<0.01 ***=<.001

elderly population in general. Table 4.9 offers some confirmatory evidence of this difference in deprivation on the housing index as it shows that rural households are significantly more likely to experience dampness and rotting floors and windows than urban households.

Do we see a similar effect when we compare single person elderly households to other types? Going back to table 4.8, we saw that the picture is fairly mixed with the single elderly only being more deprived than couples or other types of households in rural areas. However, tests show that this difference is only significant on the housing index (and only in the 'all' rather than rural or urban categories), although as table 4.10 shows, a more detailed analysis does not find any significant differences.

Table 4.10: Proportion Having Selection of Problems with Housing by Household Type (Head of Household Aged Over 64)

Type of Housing Problem	Rural	Urban	All	Sig. $\chi 2$
Lack of adequate heating	8.3	8.2	6.8	-
Damp walls, floors etc	13.6	9.4	9.7	-
Rot in windows or floors	10.8	6.3	5.9	-
Leaking roof	4.0	7.6	2.9	-
N:	324	159	206	-

Significance Key: *=<0.5 **=<0.01 ***=<.001

Identifying Elderly People Vulnerable to Deprivation

Looking at the tables so far in this chapter, it is clear that a number of factors are related to the three deprivation measures. Given this, we may have more success at seperating their individual effects if we use statistical models similar to those used at the end of the last chapter. When applying these statistical models we could look at whether particular household or individual characteristics increase or decrease deprivation. On the other hand, we could decide that deprivation is more of a discrete state, like poverty which you are either in or not. If we do the latter, we need to decide at which point on our three deprivation indexes this point arrives – i.e., when is someone deprived? Is it when they are missing one of the items from the list shown earlier (because of lack of resources), or is it two? Callan *et al.* (1993, p157) looked at this problem in relation to the 'basic' deprivation index and decided that missing one item would usually mean that the person was experiencing 'pervasive deprivation'. Given this, we adopt the same strategy here, but apply the same rule to the other dimensions of deprivation. Thus, on all of the indexes, if one or more items is absent because of a lack of resources, this is deemed to be deprivation.

As the variables we are interested in are dichotomous, i.e., households are either deprived or not, we can use the same type of logistic model as in the last chapter. Once again then we are interested in the 'odds' of people with certain characteristics being deprived compared to a 'base', or 'reference' group. Thus, just as the favorite in a horse race is given even odds (i.e. one), our reference group has odds of one and other groups have a risk greater, or smaller than this represented by odds of more than one or less than one respectively.

In the forthcoming models, we enter a limited range of variables so as to get a clear view of the basic characteristics of the elderly in deprivation. We start first with the basic deprivation measure: figure 4.1 shows the 'odds' of experiencing basic deprivation in comparison to the 'reference' category which here is urban, multi-person households with a male, non-elderly head (the full models for this chapter are available in Appendix D).

As seen already in the previous sections of this chapter, figure 4.1 shows elderly households to be significantly less likely to experience basic deprivation than households where the head is aged less than 65. Other findings are:

- Households where the head is aged over 75 are one third as likely to experience basic deprivation compared to the reference group. However, this is after controlling for the sex of the head of the household, which figure 4.1 shows has a very significant effect on the risk.
- Being female increases the risk of deprivation by 40%, thus there is a higher risk of deprivation among older women than among older men, but these women still face less risk than those in 'non-elderly' households.

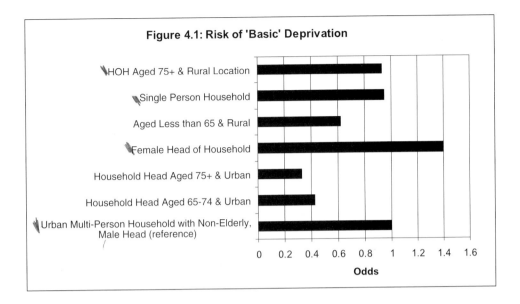

Figure 4.1: Risk of 'Basic' Deprivation

- Surprisingly, controlling for sex, age and single person status (not itself significant), those in rural locations have a lower risk than urban dwellers, although this difference in risk is almost equal if the household is headed by an over 75 and in a rural location. However, the combination of being over 74 and being in a rural location brings up the risk of being deprived from one fifth that of the under 65s in urban locales to just 7% less.

Overall, figure 4.1 confirms that the elderly and those in rural areas are at less risk of basic deprivation, but, as in the last chapter with income poverty, there is an increased risk associated with being in a household headed by a woman.

Turning to the model of the secondary deprivation index, figure 4.2 shows:

- Once again that the elderly are at no greater risk than the general population, though here there is an increased risk associated with being female and being in a rural location.
- Female-headed households are almost four times more likely to experience secondary deprivation than male headed households and those in rural locations are 1.5 times more likely than urban households.
- Being in a rural household and having a head aged between 65 and 74 increases these odds to 3.68 times those of the reference category. Thus, whereas elderly people in urban areas are at no increased risk, those between 65 and 74 in rural areas much more likely to experience secondary deprivation compared to non-elderly urban households. Although this group only make up 6% of all households, they are almost a quarter of elderly households.

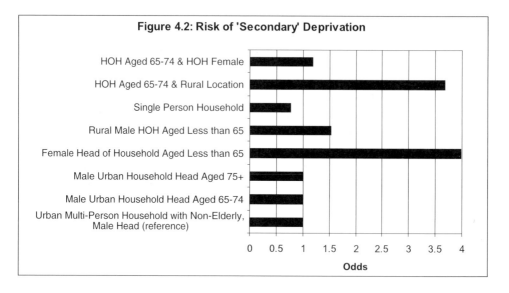

Figure 4.2: Risk of 'Secondary' Deprivation

Although 'female households' may be at a higher risk, if they are female and have a head aged between 65 and 74 this risk is reduced from almost 4 times that of non-elderly male households to 1.2 times.

In the final model of this chapter, figure 4.3, we see that:

- the elderly are at a greater risk of experiencing housing deprivation than non-elderly households. This is very much as we expected given the earlier results, and it is clear that the older the head of household the greater the risk.

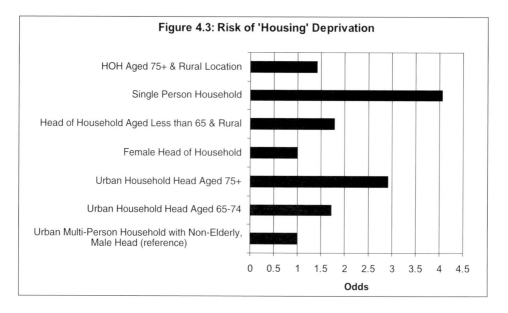

Figure 4.3: Risk of 'Housing' Deprivation

- Those in rural locations face a higher risk than urban dwellers (1.78), but unlike the results in the tables in the last section, there is a very high risk factor associated with being single after controlling for age, sex and location (over 4 times the risk of multiple person households).

This is interesting, as there was some hint of this in table 4.9, but after controlling for other relevant factors the effect appears strongly. In fact, it is this effect that accounts for the non-significance of the variable referring to the sex of the head of household as this moves into insignificance only after we enter the household size variable (not shown). This shows that in this model at least, the sex of the head of household is less of a predictor of household deprivation than being single. Lastly in this model, the interaction term between rural location and age shows that having a head of household aged over 75 attenuates the greater risk faced by those in a rural location.

Conclusions
Following the argument put forward by Ringen (1987) that income is not a good measure of poverty defined as 'exclusion from an average expected lifestyle through lack of resources', this chapter has sought to measure exclusion directly through the use of deprivation indices. The first part of the chapter showed that the 1997 Living in Ireland Survey coherently produces three latent dimensions of deprivation, *viz*, basic, secondary and housing deprivation, through questions that reflect the absence of particular items through lack of resources. The elderly are less likely to experience *basic* and *secondary* deprivation than the general Irish population, but are significantly more likely to experience *housing* deprivation. Analysis of more detailed questions on the quality of housing among the elderly showed that they were more prone to lower quality housing which was affected by dampness and structural problems.

When we examined differences in deprivation within the elderly population it became clear that, although being in a rural location and having an elderly head both protect households from basic deprivation, the rural elderly over age 75 have a higher risk. On the other hand, being in a rural location and particularly being elderly in a rural location leads to a much higher risk of secondary deprivation. This is balanced somewhat by the moderating effect that age has on the risk that being female presents for secondary deprivation. In terms of housing deprivation, those in rural locations and those in single person households are much more at risk, but having an elderly head of household in a rural location lowers one's risk compared to households headed by a person aged under 65.

Running through all the models in this chapter and the last was the increased risk of deprivation and poverty that women face compared to men. This effect comes through strongly everywhere, except in the model of household deprivation where it was masked by the large effect of being single, although the risk of being single is itself higher among the elderly population of women. This sex imbalance in risk is difficult to explain as the last chapter showed it is not simply a function of their main source of income. Even where this was controlled the effect remained, suggesting that the difference between the living standards of men and women is a deep-rooted phenomenon that is structured over a long period. If so, it is likely that such processes took root well before retirement in the economic and social situation of women. Similarly, the risk factor associated with being in a rural location suggests that on average rural living standards are lower all through the life-span and not just in old age. As the model of basic and secondary deprivation showed however, old age can exacerbate these inequalities.

Nonetheless, the findings of this chapter do not sit easily alongside those of the previous. In the next chapter we investigate how the two sets of results can be squared and put forward a more coherent overall poverty measure which takes both income and direct deprivation into account.

CHAPTER FIVE

Measuring Poverty by Combining Income and Life-Style Deprivation Information

In Chapters 3 and 4 we have analysed poverty defined in income terms and life-style deprivation. In this chapter we combine this information to produce an indicator of poverty which is consistent with the measure adopted by the National Anti-Poverty Strategy (NAPS). It is worth repeating the NAPS definition of poverty again here:

> *People are living in poverty if their income and resources (material, cultural and social) are so inadequate as to preclude them from having a standard of living which is regarded as acceptable by Irish society generally. As a result of inadequate income and resources people may be excluded and marginalised from participating in activities that are considered the norm for other people in society.*

Taking the definition of poverty as *exclusion* arising from a *lack of resources* as a starting point, the challenge is to see how information on deprivation indicators and income can be used to incorporate both exclusion and lack of resources directly into one poverty measure. Ringen's (1987) critique of reliance on income in measuring poverty is based on the argument that income is not a satisfactory measure of poverty because many of those on higher incomes suffer such deprivation in consumption and far from all the members of low income groups suffer deprivation in consumption. Therefore, if we are to make a more valid measure of poverty based on exclusion and lack of resources, the poor must be identified using both consumption/deprivation and an income criterion.

In Chapter 4 (and Appendix C) we presented the results of a factor analysis aimed at identifying the dimensions underlying the set of deprivation indicators. The results set out in Appendix C reveal a pattern similar to that found in our earlier analyses of the 1987 and 1994 data sets. It reveals three latent dimensions:

- Basic life-style deprivation – consisting of basic items such as food and clothes;

- Secondary life-style deprivation – consisting of items such as car, holidays, leisure activities.
- Housing deprivation – consisting of items relating to housing quality and facilities.

Levels of absence are generally low for the basic deprivation items and where the items are lacked this is generally considered to be enforced. The extent of possession is generally even higher for the housing items and absence is also highly likely to be attributed to lack of resources rather than choice. The secondary items are generally much less widely possessed and absence is less often considered to be enforced.

In Table 5.1 we look at the relationship between current income and the dimensions of deprivation. As in our earlier analysis we define these measures to include only those items that are available across time and income is not adjusted to take account of non-cash benefits. Looking at the figures for all households we find that income correlates highest with secondary deprivation, followed by basic with the lowest degree of association being found with the housing dimension. This pattern is consistent across time. It may seem surprising that the basic and housing indices, made up of items possessed by most of the population and regarded by most as necessities, are less highly correlated with income than the secondary dimension, which includes items much less widely held and less strongly regarded as necessities. However, this appears less surprising when we reflect on the nature of the items contained in each dimension. The housing and household capital items are of a type that will be affected by factors such as tenure arrangements and age of housing. In addition a number of the items are of a kind that would be accumulated over a long period of time, so that stage in the life-cycle and permanent income (i.e. one's average income over a number of years) would be expected to play a particularly important role. Current income would therefore be less important than it is for the items of current consumption that make up the secondary index. The items in the basic index, on the other hand, though relating largely to current

Table: 5.1: Correlation of Basic, Secondary and Housing Deprivation with Log of Equivalent Income by Household Type

	Basic Deprivation	Secondary Deprivation	Housing Deprivation
All Households	-0.28	-0.46	-0.18
Non-Elderly Households	-0.33	-0.50	-0.17
Elderly Households	-0.14	-0.33	-0.17

consumption, represent rather more extreme forms of deprivation than the secondary items. One might therefore expect that people would go to considerable lengths, drawing not only on current income, but also on savings and other accumulated resources and on available social support from extended family and friends.

Each dimension contains information about life-styles and living standards. However, in constructing our measure of poverty we focus on the basic deprivation items. As we have seen these items clearly represent socially perceived necessities and are possessed by most people. They reflect rather basic aspects of current material deprivation, and they cluster together, which lends support to the notion that they are useful indicators of the underlying generalised deprivation we are trying to measure.

Most of the items in the secondary index, on the other hand, are not overwhelmingly regarded as necessities. The housing and durables items are possessed by most households and are regarded as necessities by almost everyone, but they have a very weak relationship to current income. The correlation between the basic and housing deprivation dimensions is only 0.21 indicating that rather different household and causal processes are involved. Deprivation in terms of housing and related variables appears to be a product of very specific factors and so the housing items, though providing valuable information about one aspect of living standards, are not satisfactory as indicators of current generalised exclusion.

In Chapter 4 we saw that elderly households displayed significantly higher levels of housing deprivation, although they were no more deprived on the basic and secondary indices. An argument could thus be made that the household items should be included in our combined poverty index as this would more accurately reflect the situation of the elderly, perhaps because of the fact that it would increase the proportion of elderly under the threshold. However, the main conceptual criteria are that the relationship between the deprivation/consumption measure and that of resources be explicable through some identifiable process (i.e., not being able to buy particular items/services) and that the items in the index are popularly seen as necessities. As Chapter 4 showed, the housing items are seen as necessities, but table 5.1 also shows that the housing index is the least correlated with current income. The reasons for this were just discussed, i.e. that housing reflects tenure type and age of housing (and age of the occupants) rather than current resources. Thus, even though the correlation between current income and the basic deprivation index is lower among the elderly, the need for a generally applicable measure, plus the fact that it satisfies our other two criteria mean that the basic index is a better alternative.

The first stage in locating households excluded because of lack of resources is to identify those reporting an enforced lack of a basic item. We must also however, deal with the fact that some of those reporting enforced absence of such items are on relatively high incomes. Enforcement owing to lack of resources needs to be related to societal rather than simply individual standards and expectations. This provides the rationale for focusing on those households that are experiencing both basic deprivation and relatively low incomes. One is faced with the question of what is low income? There can of course be no unequivocal answer to this question. However, our earlier analysis suggested that the choice was between the fifty per cent and sixty per cent lines. In 1994 combining the income line criteria with the basic deprivation condition identified 9% and 14% of households respectively depending on whether the 50% or 60% income line is employed. It is on these households that the NAPS was intended to focus. At the same time it recognised that that there are other households who were income poor but who currently had resources they could draw upon and whose needs should be addressed to the extent that their position should not be allowed to deteriorate. (Sharing in Progress; National Anti Poverty Strategy, 1997:33)

Elderly Households and Combined Income and Deprivation Poverty
In this section we compare results using a combined income and deprivation poverty line with simple income poverty lines as used in chapter 3. For that purpose it is not crucial whether we combine basic deprivation with the 50% or 60% income line. Since the former creates what we would consider to be an unduly restrictive poverty line we opt for the latter. In Table 5.2 we break down poverty rates for elderly and non-elderly households for the combined income and deprivation line and for the 50% and 60% per cent relative income lines before and after adjusting for non-cash benefits. Overall the combined line gives

Table 5.2: Poverty Rates for Elderly and Non-Elderly Households Using Income Poverty Lines, Adj. Income Lines and a Combined Deprivation/Income Measure

	Combined Deprivation and Income Line	50% Income Line	60% Income Line	50% Line Adjusted for NCB	60% Line Adjusted for NCB
Non-Elderly Households	9.9	19.7	29.0	19.4	29.8
Elderly Households	9.9	28.4	59.2	12.5	54.5
All Households	9.9	21.7	36.9	17.8	35.6

poverty rates that are significantly lower than those provided by the income poverty lines. Looking at the results for 'all households' at the bottom of table 5.2, the combined measure poverty rate of 9.9% is just less than half that for the 50% income poverty line (21.7%) and less than one third of that associated with the 60% line for the total population (36.9%). The contrast in the results provided by the two approaches is greater for elderly than for non-elderly households. For the combined line the poverty rate for elderly and non-elderly households is identical whereas for the income lines the rate of poverty is significantly higher for elderly households with the gap widening as one goes from the 50% to the 60% income line. Focusing on adjusted income makes little difference when we are concerned with the 60%. Line. However, for the 50 % line the poverty rate for the elderly is significantly lower than for the non-elderly and comes fairly close to that obtained using the combined basic deprivation and 60% income line.

Our conclusions relating to poverty rates for elderly households are much more dependent on the method we use than is the case for non-elderly households. The following somewhat complicated picture emerges.

- When we focus on income lines unadjusted for cash benefits elderly households are consistently poorer. This gap widens sharply as we move from the 50% to the 60% line.
- For the adjusted income lines the picture is mixed. At the 50% line elderly households have a lower poverty rate but at the 60% line they have a significantly higher rate.
- Using the combined income and deprivation approach the risk of poverty is identical for both types of households.

The results are consistent with the earlier argument that current income is a poorer measure of command over resources for elderly households. Even if we adjust the incomes of the elderly for non-cash benefits (and probably over adjust to a degree), the effect on a combined poverty measure is marginal because the elderly are fairly well protected from extreme deprivation, even though they have relatively modest incomes.

In order to understand the discrepancies between the combined income and deprivation approach and the relative income approach it is useful to set out, as we do in Table 5.3, the nature of the inconsistencies between the two measures. For the elderly these are very substantial. One in ten households fall into the consistently poor category and four out of ten into the consistently non-poor category. The remaining one in two households exhibit inconsistency. The vast bulk of these fall into the income poor only category. Less than 2% are experiencing basic deprivation but are not below the income line. Looking at this

Table 5.3: Income Poverty and Deprivation Poverty Consistency

	Non-Elderly Households	Elderly Households	All Households
Income and Deprivation Poor	9.9	9.9	9.9
Income Poor Only	19.1	49.3	27.1
Deprivation Poor Only	6.4	1.7	5.0
Neither	64.6	39.1	58.0
Total	100.0	100.0	100.0

from another perspective we find that while over eight out of ten elderly households who experience basic deprivation are also below the 50% income line only one in six households falling below the income threshold also meet the deprivation criterion. Substituting income adjusted for non-cash benefits does not increase the level of consistency. Thus the discrepancies we observe are not simply a consequence of our choice of income measure but reflect the weak relationship between income and basic deprivation for the elderly irrespective of the income measure chosen In contrast with the elderly only one in four non-elderly households fall into the inconsistent categories. Furthermore while income only poverty is three times more frequent than deprivation poverty the balance is still a good deal more even than in the case of elderly households.

From Table 5.4 we can that there is relatively little variation in risk of poverty across household type. For households where the HOH is aged seventy five or more the poverty rate rises to 12% in comparison with the figure of 8% for households aged between sixty-five and seventy four. Within non-elderly

Table 5.4: Risk of Combined Income and Deprivation Poverty by Household Type

Household Composition	
Non-elderly Households with Children	11.8
Non-elderly Households Without Children	8.3
Household Head 65-74	7.9
Household Head >74	11.9
HOH <65 & 1+ Elderly	8.2

households a similar pattern exists for households with and without children. The range of variation, however, remains very modest.

Combined Income and Deprivation Poverty by Dependence on Income Sources

At this point it may be useful to look at the impact of household reliance on various types of income among the elderly on poverty risk for the various types of poverty line we have been considering. As before, reliance means that a household draws two-thirds or more of its income from that source. The sources we consider are old age contributory pension (OACP), old age non-contributory pension (OANCP), widow's contributory pension (WCP) and occupational pensions (OCC).[1] At the 50% income line we can see that those households dependent on old age contributory pensions display poverty rates that are only marginally higher than the overall rate. Dependence on the old age non-contributory pension or the widow's contributory pension is associated with dramatically higher poverty rates with six out of ten and seven out of ten households respectively falling below the threshold. As one moves to the 60% line these rates climb significantly so that the vast bulk of those dependent on old age non-contributory pensions and widow contributory pensions fall below this line and the rates for those relying on the old age contributory pensions and occupational pensions rise to seven out of ten and one in three respectively. Once again though, the combined income and poverty line offers a very different perspective. Using this measure only, just under one in four households reliant on old age non-contributory pensions fall below the line. Those households relying on widow's contributory pension have a rate only marginally above

Table 5.5: Poverty Rate by Reliance On Source of Income for Elderly Households

	50% Income Line	60% Income Line	Combined Deprivation and Income Line	50% Adjusted Income Line	60% Adjusted Income Line
			Percentage Poor		
OACP	16.1	68.6	6.5	4.4	56.2
OANCP	59.8	95.7	22.8	18.5	95.7
WCP	69.9	88.1	11.9	14.3	86.7
OCC	14.3	34.1	4.9	12.2	34.1

[1] We exclude widow's non-contributory pension because the numbers are rather small.

average and those on old age contributory and occupational pensions have below average rates.

The adjusted 50% income line provides a rather similar picture although the rate for those reliant on occupational pensions is significantly higher. As before, the rates for the adjusted 60% income line do not differ significantly from the corresponding 50% line. At every line it is the households reliant on old age non-contributory pensions and the widow's contributory pension who display the highest poverty rates.

However, while for the conventional relative income measures such households record poverty rates that are hugely higher than those found for non-elderly households, when we focus on the combined income and deprivation lines and the 50% line adjusted for non-cash benefits, the poverty rates for such households look much less distinctive. For those households reliant on old age contributory pensions and occupational pensions an evaluation of whether they are better off or worse off than non-elderly households is contingent upon the type of poverty line chosen.

Multivariate Analysis of the Determinants of Combined Income and Deprivation Poverty

Figure 5.1 examines the influence of a range of socio-demographic variables on the risk of falling below the 60% income line while at the same experiencing basic deprivation (the NAPS poverty line). A logistic regression, as we noted

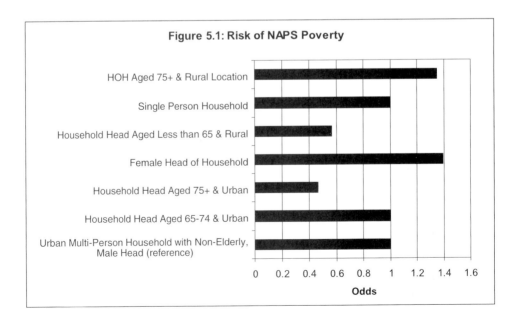

Figure 5.1: Risk of NAPS Poverty

earlier shows the 'odds' of one group of people having some characteristic (which here is being in poverty), compared to a reference group. Thus the results in figure 5.1 are the 'odds' of being poor that one group face compared to the reference group (the full model is available in Appendix E). If the score is larger than 1 they face a greater risk and if less than one, a smaller risk.

From figure 5.1 we can see that female-headed households have a somewhat greater risk of being in NAPS poverty. On the other hand there is no significant difference between single person and multi-person households. For those headed by a person aged between sixty-five and seventy four the odds of being poor do not differ significantly from those for non-elderly households. Although both having a head of household aged over 74 and living in a rural location decrease the risk of NAPS poverty, in combination they actually increase the risk as shown by the top bar in figure 5.1. This means that the impact of rural location is different for households where the household head is aged seventy-five or over from that where she/he is younger in rural locations. In the latter case the impact of rural location is to further reduce the odds of being NAPS poor. Thus in order to understand the impact of urban-rural location we must specify the age group involved and correspondingly the impact of age depends on location.

Conclusions
In this chapter we have documented an approach to the measurement of poverty that combines income and life-style deprivation information. Our objective has been to construct a measure consistent with the notion of poverty as *exclusion* arising from a *lack of resources*. We have developed the argument that such a measure should be based on the items contained in the index of basic deprivation. This was done in the light of available information relating to the degree of correlation between income, the deprivation dimensions and perceptions of social necessities. An examination of this evidence did not suggest that a different approach should be taken with the elderly.

Using the combined income and deprivation poverty line we found that elderly households have a similar risk of poverty to non-elderly households. This contrasts with the picture observed with the relative income line approach where elderly households are significantly poorer than non-elderly and this gap widens as we move from the 50% to the 60% line. Using income lines that have been adjusted for non-cash benefits gives an outcome that lies between those deriving from the earlier approaches. At the 50% line the elderly experience lower rates of poverty but the results for the 60% line are almost identical to those found using unadjusted income with the elderly having substantially higher risks of poverty. The combined results suggest that the elderly households manage to avoid extremes of deprivation despite having relatively low incomes. Almost one in two households who fall below the 60% per cent income line do not experience basic deprivation, although we should not forget that this means that one in two experience both income and deprivation poverty. While non-cash benefits provide part of the explanation it also seems likely that patterns of consumption and social support may also play a role.

CHAPTER SIX

Trends In Income Poverty and Material Deprivation 1987-97

The last three chapters have built up a complicated picture of the material standard of living of the over 65s in Ireland. On the one hand, Chapter 3 showed that the incomes of the elderly fall deep into the lower half of the national household income distribution and that this translates into poverty rates at the 50 and 60% levels which are higher than non-elderly households. The one positive feature brought out of these analyses of income was that the elderly seemed to be protected from the most severe forms of income poverty and so were under represented in the bottom 10% of the distribution. These findings tend to suggest that the lifestyles of the elderly are falling far behind those of the general population and that that their quality of life will be damaged because of this. Yet, when we turned to Chapter 4, evidence on the levels of various types of enforced deprivation among the elderly showed that in terms of *basic* and *secondary* deprivation at least, the situation of the elderly was similar to that of the rest of the population. On the other hand, levels of *housing* deprivation (i.e. lacking certain housing amenities, not lacking housing itself) were higher than among other types of households and the general state of repair was worse.

At first glance it is difficult to reconcile the stories these chapters give us, but Chapter 5 offered the beginnings of an explanation for the discrepancy by showing that the relationship between present income and both the basic and secondary deprivation indices is weakest among the elderly. Several reasons were offered for these weak relationships. It was argued that basic index, although reflecting current consumption, also represented a rather extreme form of deprivation. Because of this, we would expect people to go to considerable lengths to maintain these aspects of lifestyle, drawing not only on current income, but also on savings and other accumulated resources and on available social support from extended families and friends. This process would be particularly prevalent among the elderly. The secondary index on the other hand reflects the kind of items that would be accumulated over a longer period, thus would bear a far stronger relationship to permanent income.

However, although useful these can be only a partial explanation as the depth of income poverty among the elderly observed would suggest that both processes would be insufficient to maintain lifestyles for the overwhelming majority for an extended period. As this chapter will show, a more complete explanation needs to contextualise the findings of Chapters 3 and 4 within developments in the Irish economy in the 1990s and the relationship of a relative concept of poverty to these. This chapter will analyze trends in income poverty and material deprivation in the period from 1987 to 1997 and show how the results of these developments structure the rates of poverty using the National Anti-Poverty combined measure.

Income Poverty Lines and the Irish Experience 1987-97

It has been argued in this report that best conceptualization of income poverty is as a *relative* phenomenon. This is best summed up in the now famous quote from Peter Townsend:

> *Individuals, families and groups in the population can be said to be in poverty when they lack the resources to obtain the type of diet, participate in the activities and have the living conditions and amenities which are customary, or at least widely encouraged, or approved, in the societies to which they belong. Their resources are so seriously below those commanded by the average individual or family that they are, in effect, excluded from ordinary living patterns, customs and activities (Townsend, 1979).*

Adopting such a stance has consequences however in periods of strong growth in the economy if your interest is in the income levels of particular groups whose source of income may not be indexed against average salaries from employment. For these types of groups it is possible that real growth in income may actually translate into a worsening relative position vis-à-vis the general population. This is exactly the position of those living on state pensions between 1987 and 1997.

During this period, but particularly after 1994, strong growth in average wages and salaries combined with low inflation and tax reductions has led to a large general increase in real household disposable incomes.

As table 6.1 shows, the Irish National Accounts show fluctuating, but strong growth year to year over the decade between 1987 and 1997. Growth occurred in two major phases, the first around 1989 to 1990 and the second after 1993. Between 1987 and 1990, growth rates actually reached 7% before slipping back in a period of global recession until 1993, but overall these were years of substantial growth. As table 6.1 makes clear, the period after 1993 was one of remarkable growth by any standard which was accompanied by relatively low price inflation as measured by the CPI (or in fact GNP or GDP deflators). Between 1987 and 1994, GNP rose by 34%, but this almost doubled between 1994 and 1997 such that by 1997, real GNP per head had risen by over 61% from 1987 and GDP by almost 78%.

Table 6.1: Annual Change in Real Gross National Product, Gross Domestic Product and GNP per Head in Consumer Prices 1987-97

Year	GNP*	GDP*	GNP Per head*	CPI
		% Change In Constant Prices		% Change
1988	2.5	4.5	3.0	2.1
1989	5.4	6.3	6.0	4.0
1990	7.3	7.1	7.4	3.4
1991	2.9	1.3	1.4	3.2
1992	2.3	3.8	1.4	3.0
1993	2.7	2.8	2.6	1.5
1994	7.4	6.7	7.1	2.4
1987-94	34.6	37.2	32.5	21.3
1995	8.8	10.4	8.3	2.5
1996	6.0	7.1	5.3	1.7
1997	7.7	9.5	6.7	1.5
1987-97	67.2	77.6	61.2	28.5

*Based on average of income and output constant price series.
Source: National Income and Expenditure, 1995 & 1997, Tables A & B.

Although these figures are startling, our main interest here is in levels of income at the household level and how these changed between 1987 and 1997. We also need to examine how these levels of income differed between groups. Aggregate data on income going to households and 'private non-profit institutions' is available in the national accounts, but figures are not given for different types of households, thus here we examine income changes using data from data collected by the ESRI.

Figure 6.1 shows real levels of growth in household disposable income, equivalised[1] for household size according to the 'main source' of household income between 1987 and 1997. The main source of income is defined as that

---

[1] The equivalence scale used here and throughout this paper weights each additional adult by .66 and each child by .33. This weighting is broadly the same as that used in the Irish social security payment rates. Other weighting schemes were applied (1/.7/.5; 1/.6/.4; 1/.5/.3) to test for sensitivity but did not effect the overall results.

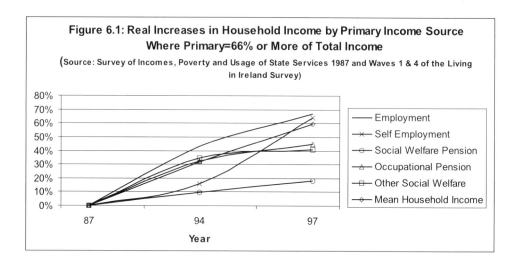

Figure 6.1: Real Increases in Household Income by Primary Income Source Where Primary=66% or More of Total Income

(Source: Survey of Incomes, Poverty and Usage of State Services 1987 and Waves 1 & 4 of the Living in Ireland Survey)

which provides 66% or more of household disposable income. The line representing growth in mean household income in figure 6.1 confirms the findings of table 6.1 in that average household income rises by around 60% between 1987 and 1997, but there are large differences in the income growth rates between different groups.

In households where the main source of income is employment, disposable income rose by over 67% between 1987 and 1997, an increase closely shadowed by those on self-employment incomes that rose by around 64% in the same period. On the other hand, those on non-market incomes such as unemployment benefits or old age pensions saw an increase in real incomes, but of 41% and 18% respectively. Some of the reason for this can be gleaned from table 6.2 which shows the rates of increase in both the contributory and means tested pensions and unemployment payments between 1987 and 1998. Although table 6.2 shows large increases in the levels of means tested unemployment benefits in the period up to 1990, rates after that are the same or lower than those for the other payment types with increases of between 0 and 3.5%. The only yearly increase outside this range was in contributory benefits in 1994 which received a larger than average rise so as to maintain parity with means tested unemployment benefits.

Compared to market incomes then, rates of increase in non-market incomes were of a substantially smaller magnitude and the increases that did occur tended to in the period before 1994. Moreover, figure 6.1 and table 6.2 both emphasise the slow rate of income growth among the elderly after 1987, although table 6.2 shows that the increase in pensions in 1998 improved matters. Nonetheless this increase will not be sufficient to make up for the low rates of increase

Table 6.2: Real Growth Rates in Contributory and Means Tested Unemployment Benefits and Old Age Pensions 1987-97

	State Payment Type			
Year	Contributory Pension	Means Tested Pension	Contributory Unemployment Benefit	Means Tested Unemployment Benefit
1988	1.0	0.9	1.0	9.0
1989	-1.1	-1.0	-0.9	7.8
1990	1.8	2.7	3.4	7.3
1991	0.9	0.6	1.0	2.6
1992	1.0	0.9	2.9	0.9
1993	2.1	2.1	3.5	2.1
1994	0.7	0.7	7.4	0.7
1995	0.0	0.0	0.0	0.0
1996	1.3	1.5	1.5	1.5
1997	2.5	3.2	3.2	3.2
1998	3.3	4.3	1.3	1.3

throughout the early 90s. Average equivalised household income (across households) has risen by almost 84% between 1987 and 1997 (£85.37 to £156.96). Taking the Old Age Contributory Pension as an example, to have kept pace with average household incomes, this would have to have been worth £101.32 in 1997 compared to the actual rate of £78 at full rate. Given these developments in the incomes of elderly people, what patterns do we see in the development of income poverty rates among the elderly over this same period?

The Development of Income Poverty Rates 1987-97

As shown in Chapter three, the inclusion of non-cash benefits has a significant impact on levels of income poverty. However, in this chapter we will confine ourselves to analyses of unadjusted income for two reasons. First of all, the methodology for imputing a value for non-cash benefits is still under-developed and we would not have complete confidence in using these estimates. Secondly, and more importantly, in this chapter we will also be assessing the development of the components which make up the National Anti-Poverty Strategy measure of poverty which does not adjust for non-cash benefits. Given the analyses in

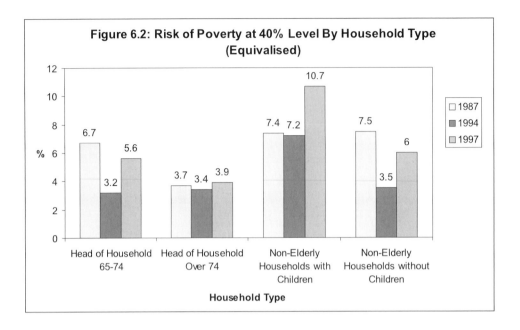

Figure 6.2: Risk of Poverty at 40% Level By Household Type (Equivalised)

chapter three, this decision only really affects the proportions of elderly under the 50% income poverty line, thus it may be useful to bear this in mind when examining the figures on 50% income poverty in this chapter.

Figure 6.2 shows the development of income poverty rates if we set the poverty rate at 40% of mean household income averaged over households. Figure 6.2 once again emphasizes that elderly households have been fairly well protected from the most severe forms of income poverty and this is true right through the period from 1987. Rates for the two types of households headed by an over 65 are consistently lower than for non-elderly households. Interestingly, although rates of income poverty fell among all groups between 1987 and 1994, they have since risen again, especially among non-elderly households with children.

Figure 6.3 shows the development of rates of income poverty at the 50% level. Bearing in mind previous comments about the effect of non-cash benefits on disposable income, the graph clearly shows the emergence of an income disparity between elderly households and non-elderly households. This process begins between 1987 and 94, but is most evident in the period between 94 and 97. Indeed, whereas rates among the two elderly household types more than double in this period, rates for non-elderly households with children actually fall by three points.

Figure 6.4 shows a similar growth in income poverty rates at the 60% level among elderly groups between 1987 and 1997, although this time, the largest proportional growth was between 1987 and 1994. Even though we have already

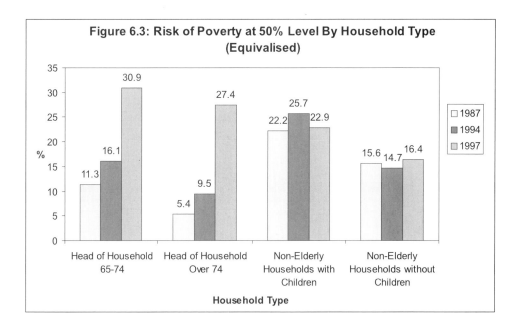

Figure 6.3: Risk of Poverty at 50% Level By Household Type (Equivalised)

seen the figures for 1997 in Chapter 3, the large proportion of elderly households below the 60% income line is still startling, particularly among the over 74's who would tend to be single, or widowed elderly women. Overall, we can see from the last three figures that the income position of those over 65 has worsened quite dramatically since 1987 relative to other groups, even though elderly incomes themselves have increased in real terms over the period.

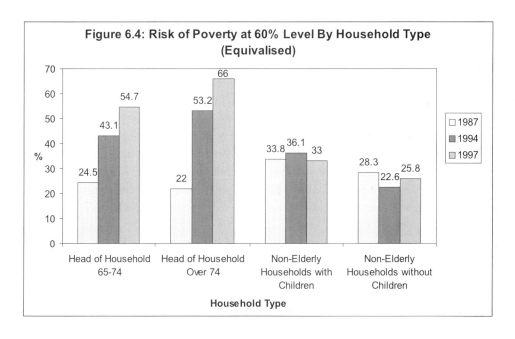

Figure 6.4: Risk of Poverty at 60% Level By Household Type (Equivalised)

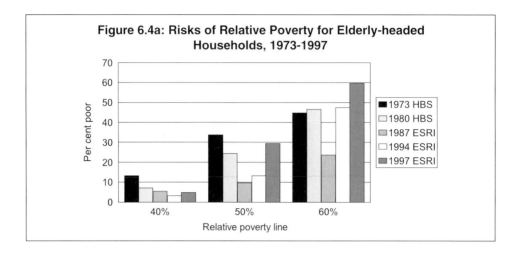

Figure 6.4a: Risks of Relative Poverty for Elderly-headed Households, 1973-1997

Developments in Income Poverty Since 1973

Although pension incomes have been losing ground relative to average employment and self-employment incomes since 1987, this is the opposite of the trend up to 1987. As figure 6.4a shows, poverty among the elderly fell dramatically between 1973 and 1987.

The incomes of the elderly increased substantially in the period after 1973 and grew much faster than the population average. Although the real value of social welfare pensions only rose by 17% between 1980 and 1987, they rose 107% over the period from 1973 to 1987. In contrast real average industrial earnings rose by 6% between 1980 and 1987 and 88% between 1973 and 1987 (Callan *et al.*, 1989, p98).

Figure 6.4b shows that 1987 actually marked the lowest point in income poverty rates among the elderly (at the 50% mean household income level) and that rates grew particularly strongly after 1994. On the other hand, among non-elderly households, figure 6.4b shows that levels of 50% income poverty remained fairly static until 1987 and then rose, although not as sharply as among the elderly.

Over a longer run period it is plain that the late 1990s represent a particularly low point for elderly incomes relative to the general population.

Material Deprivation 1987-97

Beginning first with the basic deprivation index validated in chapter 4, figure 6.5 shows the mean scores for different types of elderly and non-elderly households over the period 1987 to 1997. The picture provided by figure 6.5 is one of change among all household types over the period, all toward decreasing basic deprivation. In interpreting these changes, it is useful to bear in mind that the

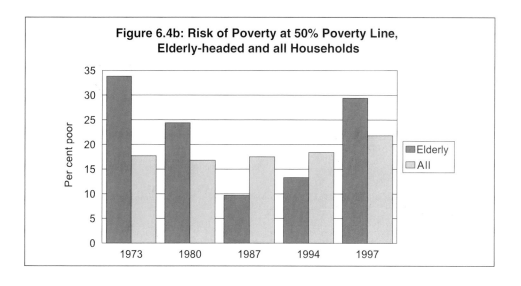

Figure 6.4b: Risk of Poverty at 50% Poverty Line, Elderly-headed and all Households

'basic' index represents quite extreme deprivation (e.g. not being able to heat one's home, eat a meal or have two pairs of shoes through lack of resources). As such, these changes among the elderly are very significant and do not suggest that the group as a whole is maintaining a particular lifestyle against a worsening economic position. If levels of basic deprivation had remained static over the

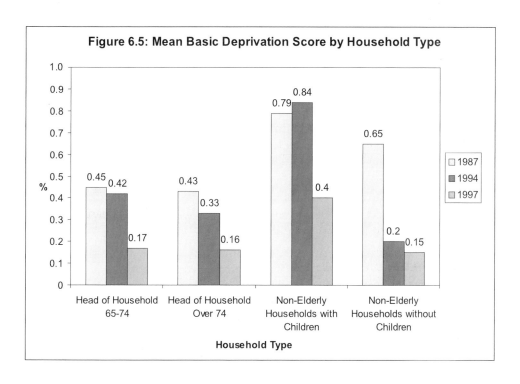

Figure 6.5: Mean Basic Deprivation Score by Household Type

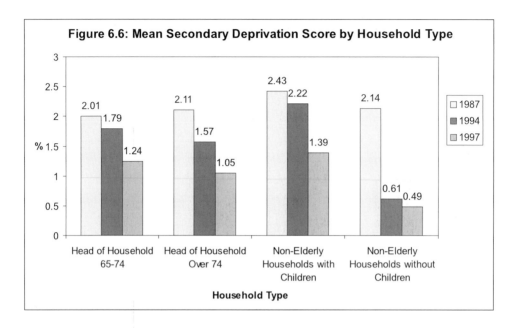

Figure 6.6: Mean Secondary Deprivation Score by Household Type

decade, it could be argued that elderly people are drawing upon savings to make up for the shortfall in incomes. However, as shown by figure 6.6, levels of deprivation actually fall over the period. Analyses of the proportion missing one or more items on the basic index show that this number has also more than halved in both elderly groups between 1987 and 1997. If basic deprivation has decreased over the period, what has happened with secondary deprivation?

Once again, figure 6.6 shows that the two household types led by elderly people have experienced a significant fall in deprivation on the secondary index. Deprivation among 'younger' elderly households (65-69) has dropped by almost 40% between 1987 and 1997 and by almost half among the older group. Interestingly, non-elderly households without children have dramatically decreased their secondary deprivation in a similar manner to the fall we saw in figure 6.5 with basic deprivation. It may be that this group made up mostly of young single adults or young couples have been in a relatively good position since 1987.

Lastly in this section, we move on to developments in deprivation on the housing index. Chapter 4 showed that this index was the only one on which the elderly appeared worse than non-elderly groups, but was this always so, or has this come about in the period between 1987 and 1997?

If anything, figure 6.7 confirms the picture we have already seen in the other two deprivation indices in terms of steady, positive improvement in the position of

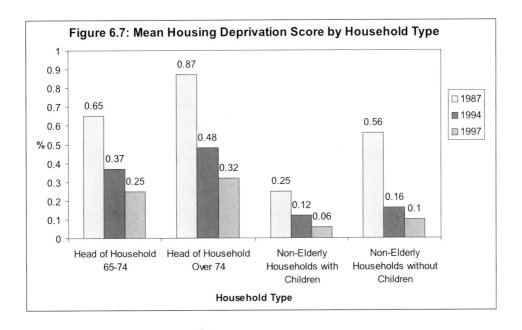

Figure 6.7: Mean Housing Deprivation Score by Household Type

the elderly. In fact the rate of improvement in the position of those households where the head is over 74 has been faster than among the same group on the basic deprivation index. Nonetheless, the housing index is the only index on which the elderly are still significantly worse off than non-elderly households. The reasons for this were discussed in Chapter 4, e.g. an older housing stock that requires more investment than most by households who are less capable of coping with the disruption necessary for structural work.

To briefly conclude this section, figures 6.5 to 6.7 suggest that the hypothesis that the elderly have maintained their lifestyles in the face of a worsening relative situation by drawing upon outside sources of income, or their own savings is unlikely to be true given that we have seen a steady decrease in deprivation over the period on all of the deprivation indices. Developments since 1987 are of the same, or even greater magnitude than other groups in Irish society. This suggests that real living standards among the elderly are improving and, as argued in Chapters 4 and 5, that income poverty figures need to be supplemented with information on actual material living standard if they are to have any real meaning. This is the aim of the National Anti-Poverty Strategy poverty measure. Thus it is to this that we now turn.

Change in the NAPS Index 1987-97

The development and rationale behind the NAPS poverty measure was discussed in detail in separate stages over the last three chapters. But to reiterate, it is a composite measure of income poverty at the 60% level and basic material

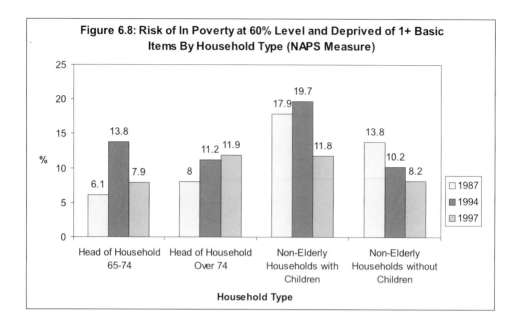

Figure 6.8: Risk of In Poverty at 60% Level and Deprived of 1+ Basic Items By Household Type (NAPS Measure)

deprivation. Thus, the NAPS, or combined poverty measure as it has come to be known is defined as missing one or more of the items on the basic index because of lack of resources and being under the 60% income poverty line.

As Chapter 5 has already shown, although elderly households have a higher risk of being poor at the 60% income poverty line and a similar risk to non-elderly households of being deprived, because there is a weak relationship between income and deprivation among the elderly, this situation does not translate into higher NAPS poverty rates. A glance at figure 6.8 confirms this for 1997, but shows some interesting variation in previous years. NAPS poverty among the younger elderly households has actually fallen between 1994 and 1997, whereas among the older group it has grown slightly. On the other hand, rates among non-elderly households have fallen uniformly across the years.

Conclusion

Although income poverty rates at the 50% and 60% levels have been rising among the elderly, this masks an absolute increase in incomes in this group and actually reflects a worsening situation relative to those on employment or self-employment incomes. However, this worsening income situation has not impacted on levels of deprivation. All three of the indicators of deprivation used in this report show an improvement in levels of deprivation among the elderly in the decade between 1987 and 97. Together, and with certain other circumstances, these complicated and contradictory developments mean that the NAPS poverty measure shows remarkably little difference between elderly and non-elderly groups and some evidence of quite a large improvement in the combined poverty situation of younger elderly persons. This difference in results for the younger and older elderly groups needs to be related back to the findings of Chapters 3 and 4 which showed that single person households, and households headed by women were more likely to be income poor, and deprived on the basic index. The greater life expectancy of women means that the older age groups are predominately female who, moreover, are likely to live in single person households. These older, mostly female single households have also experienced a drop in deprivation levels as shown by figure 6.5, but have seen their relative income position deteriorate quicker than younger elderly households, leading to the roughly stable proportions in 'combined poverty'. For the younger elderly groups, as for the population at large, the NAPS poverty target of reducing 'consistent' poverty to the range 5-10% by 2007 has already been achieved. For the older elderly on the other hand there is definitely some distance left to go. We will return to the implications that these developments have for the income and deprivation situation of the elderly in Chapter 10.

CHAPTER SEVEN

Physical Health and Material Living Standards

Although life expectancy has steadily increased in Ireland and other western industrial nations since the beginning of this century, it is still unclear whether these added years of life are also accompanied by increased chronic illness and disability[1]. Epidemiological research tends to suggest that this may be so, but morbidity is notoriously difficult to measure and no consensus has as yet emerged (Markides, 1993; Crimmins *et al.*, 1994). Yet the onset of chronic illness and the transition into dependency are two of the most important role transitions and key determinants of quality of life in old age (Fahey and Murray, 1994; Bowling *et al.*, 1997). Given this, the present chapter seeks to establish the general level of physical health of the elderly population in Ireland and compare this to the population in general.

A number of researchers have suggested that low income and deprivation are related to poor health status (Townsend and Davidson, 1982; Marmot *et al.*, 1987; Davey Smith *et al.*, 1994). It is likely that this relationship is established over a long period and that there are a number of direct and indirect routes of causation (Kuh and Ben Shlomo, 1997; Mheen *et al.*, 1998). Nonetheless, socio-economic inequalities are an important aspect of the health of the elderly, thus this chapter will examine to what extent the physical health of those over 65 is related to their household resources. Lastly, we also examine the relationship between the material resources of the elderly and their use of medical services. There is evidence (Nolan, 1991) that those on low incomes are far less likely to visit a GP even when ill compared to those on higher incomes. This chapter will investigate the effect of income on their GP utilization and whether possession of a medical card negates these differences.

Measures of Morbidity
Health measurement is a notoriously difficult area (Bowling, 1991). Although there has been a great deal of development in the use of subjective health

---

[1] However, life expectancy at age 65 in Ireland in 1990 ranked lowest among 23 OECD countries for both men and women (WHO, World Health Statistics Annual 1992).

measures in recent years, illness and its impact on the person are complex and subjectively experienced in different ways by different people or groups of people. The Living in Ireland Survey (1997) contains several subjective health measures that will be used in this chapter. Questions on health in a standardized large-scale questionnaire can never completely tap the true complexity of illness and in some cases are prone to response error. Nonetheless, for all their problems, the measures used in the LIS survey have been shown in a large amount of research throughout Europe and the US to be generally reliable, especially for inter-group comparisons. The first of our measures is a general question that asks respondents to rate their health 'in general' on a scale from 'very bad' through 'fair' to 'very good'. This has been used in a large number of surveys and has been shown to be a very reliable, though simple measure of general health status (Cunny and Perry, 1991) and of risk of death (Kazis *et al.*, 1989). The questionnaire also asked if the respondent had a chronic or long-standing illness and to what degree this hampered their daily activities or restricted their mobility. The questionnaire asked respondents whether they had 'cut down on their usual activities' because of physical or mental/emotional health problems during the last two weeks.

These subjective health measures are complemented by a set of questions that ask about use of medical services including visits to hospital, general practitioners, medical specialists, dentists, and opticians in the last year. These allow us to more closely examine the relationship between income and use of medical services.

The Health Status of the Elderly
As suggested in the introduction to this chapter, evidence suggests that increasing longevity among the populations of western industrial countries is accompanied by an increase in morbidity in older age groups. Fahey and Murray (1994) found that whereas rates of morbidity among women did indeed increase in older elderly groups, men experienced higher rates of morbidity at earlier ages. On the other hand, Fahey and Murray also found that there was no age gradient in the proportions describing their health as good or very good, which suggests that people may take their age into account when assessing health and that their conception of health is thus essentially relative.

To what extent is age linked to declining health in the Irish population in the 1997 Living in Ireland Survey? Table 7.1 shows the proportions of men and women who state that they have a chronic physical or mental illness by age group.

We can see from table 7.1 that rates of chronic illness after age sixty-five are three times higher than when under age 30 and almost 5 times higher after age 71. Interestingly, rates drop after age 80 among women, and women also tend to have higher rates than men after age 71. Given that male life expectancy is

**Table 7.1: Proportion with Chronic Physical or
Mental Health Problem by Age Group**

Age Group	Men %	Women %	All %
17 to 30	11.7	9.7	10.7
31 to 50	13.3	18.6	16.0
51 to 64	28.8	23.3	26.1
65 to 69	35.8	33.1	34.4
71 to 79	37.7	56.7	48.3
80+	44.6	48.2	46.8
All 65+	38.4	47.6	43.6
All	18.7	21.2	19.9

lower, this could be attributable to the deaths at earlier ages of unhealthy men. These figures confirm that chronic illness affects a large minority of the elderly.

What effect does chronic illness have on quality of life and does this get worse in older age groups? As mentioned above, although elderly people suffer more chronic illness they also tend to have lower expectations about their capabilities and general level of health and will thus be more satisfied with their health status. We can begin to assess this question first by examining the degree to which chronic illness hampers daily activities in table 7.2. If the elderly expect to do less, this does not seem to translate into lower proportions being hindered by their chronic illness after age sixty-five in table 7.2.

Each older age group is significantly more likely to be hampered by their chronic illness than the preceding group, although even among those under thirty, over 73% are hampered to some degree. After age 71, almost 90% of those with a chronic illness will be hampered by it, almost 30% severely. Once again table 7.2 shows that those over 80 seem to be less affected by chronic illness. However, although the overall proportion hampered to some degree among this group is comparable to those between 51 and 64, almost twice as many are affected severely. It also appears that elderly men aged between 65 and 70 are more likely than women to be hampered to some degree which suggests that men may suffer more from their chronic illness.

Of course, in making these comparisons, we are making the assumption that chronic illnesses of the elderly are of the same kind as those under 65 and thus

Table 7.2: Proportion with Chronic Illness who Are Hampered in their Daily Activities by Age Group

Age Group	Men Some %	Severely %	Women Some %	Severely %	All Some %	Severely %
17 to 30	60.3	19.8	56.1	8.4	58.4	14.7
31 to 50	58.8	20.6	64.7	9.1	62.5	13.6
51 to 64	60.6	18.8	62.2	13.4	61.1	16.6
65 to 70	56.6	30.2	45.5	29.1	50.9	30.2
71 to 80	72.0	17.3	54.9	34.0	60.7	28.3
81+	43.2	40.5	47.0	27.3	45.6	32.0
All Ages	60.1	21.6	58.1	17.7	59.0	19.5

affect them in the same way. This is not necessarily so as an examination of the illnesses suffered shows that a far larger proportion of the elderly suffer from illnesses of the musculature and circulatory system which could have a far greater impact on daily activities than, say, skin diseases or emotional problems.

Table 7.3 shows the degree of disability experienced by the elderly with a chronic illness. Although only a small proportion are bedridden or wheel chair bound by their chronic illness, over 46% have some mobility problem and mobility seems to be a particular problem among elderly women.

Table 7.3: Proportion of Elderly with Chronic Illness Experiencing Particular Mobility Restrictions

Mobility Problem	Men %	Women %	All %
Confined to Bed	3.3	1.6	2.2
Wheel Chair User	3.3	5.2	4.5
Other Mobility Problems	31.6	45.2	40.1
No Mobility Problems	61.8	48.0	53.2
Total	100	100	100

Table 7.4: Proportion of Elderly 'Cutting Down on Usual Activities' Because of Physical or Mental/Emotional Health Problems

Physical or Mental/Emotional Health Problem	Men %	Women %	All %
Because of Physical Illness or Injury	13.2	18.6	16.3
Because of Emotional or Mental Health Problems	1.6	5.1	3.6

Overall then, it is clear that a large minority of the elderly suffer from some sort of chronic physical or mental illness and that these tend to hamper the daily activities of the elderly, quite often in a serious way. It could be suggested that if the elderly have grown used to such problems they will find alternative ways of doing activities that will circumvent the health problems that they have. There is some evidence of this in table 7.4, which shows the proportion of the elderly who have cut down on their usual activities in the last two weeks because of a physical or mental/emotional health problem. Whereas over 45% of the elderly have a chronic illness that hampers them to some degree, only 20% have actually cut down in the last two weeks because of this. This is an encouraging result, but we should use some caution in interpreting it as the concept of 'usual activities' may be problematic for those who have had a chronic illness for a long period. It could be for instance, that this question simply picks up short term decreases in health status.

If the elderly seem to 'normalize' their health problems to some degree, does this mean that they also come to have a concept of their overall health as 'good' in spite of their level of chronic illness? Table 7.5 shows that the proportions from

Table 7.5: Proportion Rating Health 'Good' or 'Very Good' by Age Group

Age Group	% Men		% Women		% All	
	No Illness	Illness	No Illness	Illness	No Illness	Illness
17 to 30	98.0	49.6	96.5	59.8	97.3	54.2
31 to 50	94.8	48.5	92.8	40.7	93.8	43.8
51 to 64	90.9	19.4	86.1	26.8	88.4	22.6
65 to 70	87.4	14.0	86.2	21.2	86.8	17.6
71 to 79	85.6	33.3	84.5	30.8	85.4	31.7
80+	80.4	13.5	76.1	13.6	77.8	13.6
Total	94.4	34.2	92.1	35.3	93.3	34.8

the age groupings already listed who rate their health as good or very good in answer to the general question 'all things considered, would you rate your health very good, good etc.' split by whether respondents report a chronic illness. Contrary to table 7.4, table 7.5 suggests that respondent's assessments of their health are quite closely related to whether they have a chronic illness, with chronic illness impacting more strongly on perceived health as age increases. Under 30, those with a chronic illness are half as likely to see their health as good, or very good compared to those without a chronic illness. After age 65, this drops to one fifth as likely. Thus, just as chronic illness is related to greater levels of hindrance in daily activities in the elderly compared to younger respondents, it is also associated with a greater decrease in perceived health status.

Morbidity and Material Standard of Living

In this section of the chapter we will examine whether the variation that we have witnessed so far among the elderly in the 1997 Living in Ireland Survey by age may be related to their income and deprivation position. Having established coherent measures of income and deprivation and looked at the distributions of these variables among the elderly in Chapters 3 to 5 we can now see whether they may also influence the health status of the elderly.

Income or Deprivation?

The analyses in previous chapters and particularly chapter five, have shown that the measures of disposable income and material deprivation through lack of resources reflect very different aspects of material well-being and are not necessarily highly correlated. But how are these measures related to health? Leaving aside the interaction between material circumstances, health behaviour and ill health, the causal mechanisms highlighted in the academic literature tend to be of two sorts: on the one hand, few resources and low income are said to influence health directly through material living standards. For example, lower income may decrease the quality of housing or food available to households and individuals making them more likely to experience bronchial or rheumatic problems and poor nutrition. In the same way, low socio-economic position is also associated with occupations that tend to be more dangerous or hazardous. On the other hand, poor economic position can affect health indirectly through psychological reactions such as stress that have mental health outcomes as well as psycho-somatic consequences (Kelly et al., 1997; Elstad, 1998).

For socio-economic position to affect health in either of these ways in any serious manner, we would expect that this situation would have to be experienced for a substantial period. As the discussion in chapters 3 to 5 and past research have made clear, current income is not necessarily a good measure of long term income (Nolan et al., 1994). Therefore, we can expect that a measure of present income, or income poverty is unlikely to be significantly correlated with ill health[2]. On the other hand, material deprivation through lack of resources should be a better indicator of long-term income and thus the circumstances that individuals have been faced with that may cause ill health. On this basis, we should find that those deprivation scales that reflect long term resources such as the basic or secondary indexes will be better correlates of ill health than housing deprivation which will be related to other factors such as age and building type.

To establish the association between income/deprivation and health, we will need to exclude the effects of other variables that may confound our analysis. As in previous chapters, the obvious way to do this is with a statistical model that can control for the effect of other variables as well as those that we are directly interested in. In modeling health, we have the choice of several different subjective measures, all of which have been examined in this chapter so far. We have chosen to use whether the respondent has a physical or mental chronic illness as the outcome. This was chosen in preference to the subjective measure of own health rating (i.e. 'in general, how good would you say your health is') because this should be a better proxy for actually having a medical condition and is not as affected by comparison process.

To make sure that our analysis of the probability of having a chronic illness is not influenced by other, intervening characteristics, we enter the following variables into the model:

- *Age and sex:* Table 7.1 showed that older elderly people are much more likely to have a chronic illness and also that women between 71 and 79 are more likely than men. As such, we will need to control for both these variables in the model.

- *Rural/urban location:* it may be that as well as being significantly less affluent than the average urban elderly person, elderly people in rural locations are more likely to be less healthy thus rural location is controlled for in the model.

- *Education:* education may also play a part in chronic illness. Higher educated groups tend to smoke less, eat a better diet and consume less alcohol and this may affect the probability of chronic illness. To control for this, a variable for education is entered into the model.

- *Household type:* It may be that living alone has a detrimental effect on health, thus a variable is entered to control for this status.

---

[2] It could also be suggested that relative income poverty would also be unlikely to be related to ill health since it is particular circumstance, not just one's relative position to others that is important. However, (Wilkinson, 1996) has suggested that income inequality in its own right may account for inequalities in health.

Lastly, we have a choice of different deprivation and income poverty variables that we could use in the model as predictors of health. Given the discussion above, all these will be entered into the model individually to assess their effects, although we would expect that only basic and secondary deprivation would be predictors of having a chronic illness. To make interpretation easier, the income and deprivation variables are also entered as dichotomous measures of either income poverty or missing one or more item for the index list through lack of resources.

Correlates of Ill health Among the Elderly

Figure 7.1 shows the effect of a number of significant variables from the model both alone and in combination on the odds of having a chronic illness (the full models are available in Appendix F). Figure 7.1 shows that, as already seen in this chapter, age is a risk factor in developing a chronic illness, as is being female. The latter effect is interesting as table 7.1 shows that women are actually less likely to report a chronic illness in the 'middle years' between 30 and 70. Only after this do women begin to report more chronic conditions. As in most other countries, men have a lower life expectancy than women in Ireland and as noted earlier, this may mean that we see only relatively fit men at ages over 69.

However, we are most interested in the link with the deprivation indices and figure 7.1 shows that, after controlling for age, sex, location, living alone and education, being deprived on both the basic and secondary indices (i.e. missing one or more items through lack of resources) is associated with an increased risk of chronic illness. If these risk factors are combined, the 'odds' of having a chronic illness rise quickly such that a woman aged 80+ who was deprived on both the basic and

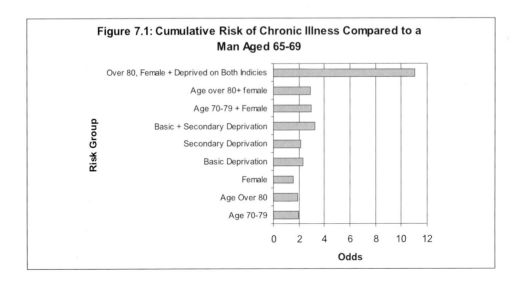

Figure 7.1: Cumulative Risk of Chronic Illness Compared to a Man Aged 65-69

secondary indices has over eleven times the risk of a man under 70 who is not deprived. Appendix F shows that living in a rural location is associated with better health when controlling for sex, age and household type, but this effect becomes insignificant when we control for poverty and deprivation status.

To conclude this section, it is clear that experiencing either basic or secondary deprivation is associated with an increased risk of chronic illness. It is probable that this effect reflects a long term lack of resources over the life course rather than a short run process. That we should have a significant effect for being female underlines the finding elsewhere in this report that women are at a material disadvantage compared to men and that this can have distinct consequences for their health and thus their quality of life.

Health, Material Circumstances and Use of Medical Services

The 1997 survey contains a range of information on the usage of medical services that would be useful in assessing the effect of health status on the quality of life of the elderly population. The main question to be addressed is whether the health needs of the elderly are being addressed and whether material resources have any impact on this. This question is especially important in the light of their levels of chronic illness as this means that the elderly have greater need of medical services than the majority of the population.

Table 7.6 shows the proportion admitted to hospital in the last 12 months by age group (on own account). Although rates of admittance among women aged 65 to 69 are actually lower than those of women aged under 30, the general pattern is for

Table 7.6: Proportion Admitted to Hospital in Last Year by Age Group

Age Group	Men %	Women %	All %
17 to 30	8.0	16.4	12.1
31 to 50	7.9	14.0	11.0
51 to 64	12.4	10.3	11.4
65 to 69	19.0	13.5	16.1
71 to 79	19.0	25.3	22.3
80+	39.0	34.1	35.9
All Elderly	22.8	24.0	23.4
Total	10.6	15.7	13.2

Table 7.7: Selected Variables by Age Group and Sex

Age Group	Sex	Mean No. Nights in Hospital Last Year	Mean Consultations with GP	% Consulting a GP 1 or More Times in Last Year
	Men	2.86	5.35	82.3
65-69	Women	1.32	6.27	95.1
	All	2.05	5.84	89.1
	Men	2.18	5.10	92.5
70-79	Women	3.86	6.75	95.3
	All	3.12	6.02	94.0
	Men	11.08	7.19	90.4
80+	Women	5.69	7.24	94.5
	All	7.73	7.22	93.5
	Men	4.13	5.59	88.6
All	Women	3.56	6.73	95.1
	All	3.81	6.23	92.3

rates to rise after age 65. Over a third of all elderly aged 80+ have been admitted to hospital in the last year and one in four of people aged over 65. This is a very large significant proportion of the elderly and bespeaks a high level of need.

Table 7.7 lists the average number of consultations with a general practitioner in the last year, the number of nights spent in hospital in the last year, and the proportion paying any visit to a GP in the last year by age and sex. The first column shows that the number of nights spent in hospital in the last year rise quickly with age and leap after age 79, particularly among men. Similarly, the number of visits to the GP rise steadily from an average of 5.8 among the 65 to 69 year olds to 7.22 among the 80 age group. Interestingly, men seem to consult the GP less than women throughout the elderly age range. The question is however, how are these patterns of consultation affected by socio-economic circumstances?

In Ireland the costs of medical treatment from general practitioners, outpatient services, public clinics and in hospitals is borne by the users except in certain circumstances. The structure of entitlement to free or subsidized medical care from the State is a central element in the Irish system of health care. Groups entitled to free care are those unable, without undue hardship, to arrange general practitioner, medical and surgical services for themselves and their dependents. People in this situation are entitled to a 'medical card'. The medical card gives full eligibility to all health services free of charge including GP care, prescribed drugs, out-patient and in-patient care in public hospitals. Individuals or households without a medical card have to pay for treatment either directly, or

Table 7.8: Proportion with Access to a Medical Card by whether Elderly

	% Aged Under 65	% Elderly	% All
Holder	21.9	58.9	27.2
Covered on Someone Else's	6.5	10.6	7.0
Not Covered	71.7	30.5	65.8
Total	100	100	100

through private health insurance except in cases of acute medical need.

Table 7.8 shows the proportion of the elderly covered by a medical card either in their own right or as a dependent on a medical cardholder. Compared to the general population, a large proportion of the elderly are covered such that less than one third have no access to free medical care.

In contrast, the proportion of elderly with medical insurance is substantially smaller than among the non-elderly. However if we cross-tabulate having a medical card with medical insurance in table 7.10, 11% of the elderly population have neither private, nor state medical cover. Although compared to the rest of the Irish population this is relatively small proportion, it still represents over 40,000 people in 1997.

Table 7.9: Proportion Covered by Private Medical Insurance by Whether Elderly

	Aged Under 65	Aged 65+	All
% Covered By Medical Insurance	42.7	25.3	40.2

7.10: Proportion of Elderly with Medical Card and/or Private Medical Insurance

Have Medical Card?	Medically Insured?		
	No	Yes	Total
No	10.8	19.8	30.7
Yes	63.8	5.5	69.3
Total	74.7	25.3	100%

Table 7.11: Access to Medical Card by Mean Consultations with GP

	Holder	Covered on Someone Else's	Not Covered	All
Mean Consultations with GP	7.39	7.25	3.64	6.23

Although medical insurance would tend to cover out-patient or in-stay periods and treatment in hospital, it does not cover visits to the GP, thus does the lack of a medical card to cover this expense lead to less utilization of GP services among this group? Table 7.11 would tend to suggest that it does given that those without a medical card had substantially fewer visits to the GP in the year before the LIS survey than those with a medical card.

However, as stated above, medical cards can be received precisely because the individual has a higher level of medical need, but cannot afford to seek treatment. The numbers receiving cards on this basis are small, but we would need to control for the health status of the person if we are to get a reliable picture of usage. To control for these factors we should examine visits to the GP within a multi-variate framework.

As the underlying variable we are modeling is the number of visits to a GP, we can use a simple linear regression model which allows us to see how certain characteristics change the number of GP visits whilst controlling for other factors such as the sex, location and health state of the individual. After controlling for all these effects, we can see what effect having a medical card has on utilization of GP services[3].

Table 7.12 shows that having a medical card is associated with an increase in the number of visits to the GP. This suggests that among the 30% or so of elderly people without a medical card, there may be at least some element of restriction in the face of chronic illness.

Conclusion

This chapter has set out to examine the health status of the elderly population in Ireland, how it differs from the general population and whether it has a large impact on quality of life. As expected from previous research we found large

---

[3] Ordinarily, we would have to control for the large number of zero visits in the population in general. However, among the elderly, table 7. 7 shows that over 92% have visited the GP in the last 12 months.

Table 7.12: OLS Model of GP Utilization Among the Those Aged Over 65

	Increase in Number of GP Visits	
Hold Medical Card	2.947	***
Have Access to Medical Card	2.568	***
Constant	1.924	***

*Key: ***=P<0.001 **=P<0.01 *=P<0.05   R²:0.18*

increases in the levels of chronic illness among older age groups. Around 44% of elderly people had a chronic physical or mental condition. Compared to younger age groups, this high level of chronic illness seemed to hamper their daily activities and almost half of those experiencing a chronic condition had mobility problems to one degree or another. This level of health problems would suggest that the quality of life of the elderly is affected quite severely. As well as impacting on mobility and routine activities, chronic illness also decreased the perceived health status of elderly people to a greater degree than among younger respondents, suggesting that the onset of chronic illness among the elderly is an important transition.

One of the main questions of the chapter though was the degree to which physical health is associated with the material standard of living and socio-economic position of the person. By modeling whether the respondent had a chronic condition we found that experiencing basic or secondary deprivation was a very significant predictor of ill health. Our theory had suggested that income on its own, or as a poverty indicator would not be useful as this would tend to be present orientated, whereas deprivation is a better indicator of long term income and access to resources.

The last part of the chapter analyzed the usage of medical services. The high levels of ill health shown earlier in the chapter were reflected in the degree of usage of medical services among the older population. Almost a quarter had been admitted to hospital in the preceding 12 months to the survey and over 90% had consulted a GP. The last part of the chapter showed that, although a smaller proportion of the elderly population have medical insurance compared to the general population, 30% lack a medical card giving them free access to medical services. However, the last table of the chapter showed the results of a multi-variate analysis which suggested that take up of GP services may be restricted among those without a medical card.

CHAPTER EIGHT

Psychological Health and Material Living Standards

The previous chapter showed that those aged over 65 carried a significant burden of ill health that impacted on their lifestyle and quality of life. On the other hand, there were signs that older people suffering from chronic illnesses did acclimatize to their condition and a large proportion still rated their health as good or very good. In this chapter, a measure of psychological stress or distress (the General Health Questionnaire) from the 1997 Living in Ireland survey is used to examine the psychological health of the over 65s. One very important area we will examine is the impact of physical ill health and chronic illness on levels of stress. As explained in the last chapter, there is a considerable amount of research into the relationship between low socio-economic position and bad physical health which uses psychological stress as the intermediate causal mechanism (Kelly *et al.*, 1997; Elstad, 1998), but in the short run, bad physical health can also be a cause of psychological stress. Pain and discomfort aside, ill health can also limit one's mobility and independence and produce uncertainty which can all increase levels of stress.

In keeping with our focus on the ramifications of material living standards for quality of life, we will also examine the impact of income poverty and resource deprivation on psychological health. In this chapter we will examine whether income poverty and resource deprivation impact on psychological health just as deprivation impacted on physical health in the last.

Measuring Psychological Distress
The General Health Questionnaire (or GHQ) is a short, self-administered survey designed to detect minor psychiatric disorders that has been adapted for use in survey questionnaires administered through interview. In the survey format, the original 60-item version is usually shortened to either a 12 item or 30-item version and it is the 12 item version which is used in the Living in Ireland Survey. Tests show that the 12-item version is as reliable as the 60-item version (although it is obviously less sensitive) as well as being appropriate for use among older people (Bowling, 1991).

The GHQ survey is made up of a list of 12 question items that ask respondents about their *present* mental and emotional condition 'over the last few weeks' in comparison to their *normal* condition. The concept of the 'normal' self is a tenuous one, especially where individuals are experiencing recurrent bouts of some illness, or have acquired a chronic illness which has been with them for some time and will continue to be. Nonetheless, research has shown that respondents do still tend to see their 'ill self' as not the 'normal' them and thus can give a reliable account of their psychological condition in general terms (Goldberg and Williams, 1998). The questions are also relative to the person concerned as they ask about deviations from the normal self and thus do not imply an absolute standard.

The questions in the version used in the 1997 Living in Ireland Survey are listed in table 8.1 along with a number representing which of two possible response sets are used for that question. These questions were part of the individual questionnaire and were thus asked of all respondents eligible and capable of giving a full interview.

In the general population, the proportions stating that they are closest to the most negative answer are usually very small, but substantial proportions can choose one of the negative categories. For instance, although only 3.7% of respondents stated that they had 'been thinking of themselves as a worthless person' rather more, or much more than usual, almost 20% report being constantly under strain rather more, or much more than usual.

Table 8.1: The General Health Questionnaire (GHQ)

"Please describe the way you have been feeling over the last few week..."

1	Been able to concentrate on whatever you're doing?	1
2	Lost much sleep over worry?	2
3	Felt you were playing a useful part in things?	1
4	Felt capable of making decisions about things?	1
5	Felt constantly under strain?	2
6	Felt that you couldn't overcome your difficulties?	2
7	Been able to enjoy your normal day to day activities?	1
8	Been able to face up to your problems?	1
9	Been feeling unhappy and depressed?	2
10	Been losing confidence in yourself?	2
11	Been thinking of yourself as a worthless person?	2
12	Been feeling reasonably happy, all things considered?	1

Response set 1:	*Response set 2*
More so than usual	Not at all
Same as usual	No more than usual
Less than usual	Rather more than usual
Much less than usual	Much more than usual

Table 8.2: GHQ Distress Scores Among Over 65s by Sex

GHQ Score	% Men	% Women	% All
0	58.7	51.5	54.7
1	14.5	10.7	12.4
2	7.5	8.9	8.3
3	3.6	6.9	5.4
4	2.7	3.4	3.1
5	3.8	6.1	5.1
6	1.5	0.8	1.1
7	0.6	1.6	1.1
8-12	7.2	10.1	8.7
Total	100	100	100
Mean GHQ Score	1.5	2.06	1.81

To construct a measure from these questions that can be used in analysis, we need to collapse the four possible responses to each question into two categories which reflect whether the person is feeling 'as normal' or experiencing distress above that they would normally feel. By assigning a value of 1 to choices which indicate an abnormal situation we can produce a 12 point scale upon which to compare particular groups by summing collapsed scores across the questions. In almost all studies of general populations, the majority of respondents will score zero on this scale, although a sizeable minority will score between 1 and 3. On the other hand on a small proportion should usually score over 8.

Table 8.2 lists the proportionate scores for respondents in the 1997 Living in Ireland Survey divided by sex. As expected a majority of both men and women score zero on the scale (i.e. are experiencing no more psychological distress 'than usual'), although a sizeable minority score 1 or more. One of the well known patterns from the GHQ is the tendency for women to exhibit more distress than men (Whelan *et al.*, 1991, p25) and this is apparent from the results in table 8.2, both in terms of the proportions scoring zero and the mean score.

What patterns do we see among the elderly? Table 8.3 lists the mean GHQ score of those over 65 grouped by age and sex. As in table 8.1, women generally score

Table 8.3: Mean GHQ Score of Over 65s by Age Group

Age Group	Sex	Mean GHQ	Stand. Dev.
65-69	Men	1.52	2.79
	Women	1.32	2.52
	All	1.42	2.65
70-79	Men	1.32	2.53
	Women	1.96	2.78
	All	1.67	2.69
80+	Men	1.90	2.60
	Women	3.18	3.82
	All	2.69	3.45
All Over 65	Men	1.50	2.64
	Women	2.06	3.06
	All	1.81	2.89
All under 65	Men	0.91	1.99
	Women	1.43	2.55
	All	1.19	2.32

higher than men, although this does not seem to be the case in the 65 to 69 year age group. When we look at the 'all' groups in each age group, it is apparent that as well as there being a sex differential, there is also an age progression with older groups experiencing higher levels of psychological distress. However, only the 80+ age group is significantly different from the two younger groups (P<0.0001).

How should we explain these elevated levels of distress among older age groups? One explanation may be the increased levels of illness and particularly chronic illness suffered by those over 64. Illness may not though explain all of the increase. Previous work has shown that living circumstances may contribute to psychological stress with those living alone, and particularly those who were married, but are now widowed experiencing higher levels of distress. Another very important contributor in the context of this report is stress caused by low income and lack of resources. If we are to unpack the levels of distress among the elderly we should examine all these possible sources of variation. However, before doing that, it may be useful to introduce an innovation in the presentation of GHQ scores that will help us present the information more clearly.

Research on the GHQ has shown that if we compare scores with clinical diagnoses, there is a point on the scale where the probability of diagnosis of a psychiatric disturbance rises to at least 0.5 or more. Thus, if we were to present all those with a score above this threshold to a clinician, on average one half

Table 8.4: Proportion Over GHQ Threshold by Age and Sex

Age Group	Men	Women	All
17-30	11.3	19.4	15.6
31-50	12.2	19.2	16.0
51-64	13.7	21.2	17.3
65-69	17.4	16.9	17.1
70-79	17.7	29.1	24.0
80+	27.6	43.8	37.6
All 65+	19.4	28.9	24.7
All Under 65	12.2	19.6	16.1
All Ages	13.3	21.1	17.4

would be diagnosed with a psychiatric disturbance. Tests show that this point is reached at a score of three or more, thus we can dichotomize scores on the scale running from zero to twelve into scores under three and three or more.

Table 8.4 shows that if we apply this technique to the 1997 Living in Ireland population and examine the results by age we get a similar age progression in the proportions above the threshold as observed with mean scores on the linear

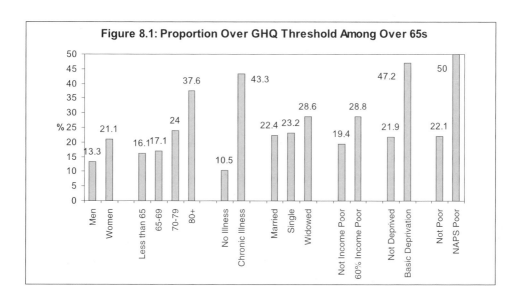

Figure 8.1: Proportion Over GHQ Threshold Among Over 65s

scale, although the progression is quite uneven among female respondents. Nonetheless, there is still a clear differentiation between younger respondents and those over 65 that suggests that this group experience rather more psychological distress (P<0.001).

Figure 8.1 shows the proportions of elderly respondents above the GHQ threshold by a number of variables that were just mentioned as possible sources of increased levels of distress. It clearly shows that age is related to increased distress, but also shows, as we suspected, that chronic illness, marital status and socio-economic status all contribute to heightened distress. As suggested before though, does their level of chronic illness explain the increased risk of over 65s to distress completely? The best way to test this is to control for chronic illness and then examine the proportions scoring over the threshold by age. Table 8.5 shows the result of this procedure.

Examining table 8.5, we don't get quite the easy answer we expected in terms of explaining the higher incidence of distress among the elderly. Although among those without a chronic illness, the proportions of over 65s over the threshold is similar or even less than the under 65s, when we look at those with an illness, there is still a clear surplus of over 65s above the threshold (P<0.01). Could it be, however, that we are not really comparing like with like when we examine the chronic illnesses of those over and under 65? As the last chapter showed, the elderly with a chronic illness were far more likely than those under 65 to be hampered by their condition and suffer mobility problems. Could this not explain the difference? Table 8.6 shows the proportions above the GHQ threshold, but this time just among those with a chronic illness and controlling for mobility problems.

Table 8.6 shows that the difference in distress between those over and under 65 is more to do with the incidence of mobility problems among the elderly with

Table 8.5: Proportion Above GHQ Threshold by Age & Chronic Illness

| Chronic Illness | Age Over 65 | % Over GHQ Threshold | | |
		No	Yes	Total
No	No	87.6	12.4	100
	Yes	89.5	10.5	100
Yes	No	63.8	36.2	100
	Yes	56.7	43.3	100

Table 8.6: Proportion of Those with a Chronic Illness Above GHQ Threshold by Age & Mobility Problems

Mobility Problems	Age Over 64	% Over GHQ Threshold		
		No	Yes	Total
No	No	67.5	32.5	100
	Yes	67.4	32.6	100
Yes	No	49.4	50.6	100
	Yes	41.5	58.5	100

chronic illnesses. Among those with a chronic illness, but no mobility problems, the proportion above the threshold among older and young respondents is identical. On the other hand, when we look at those suffering mobility problems there is a significantly greater proportion of the elderly above the threshold ($P<0.05$). However, this still leaves open the question of why mobility problems have a higher impact on psychological distress among the elderly than non-elderly.

Psychological Health, Poverty and Resource Deprivation

Figure 8.1 in the last section showed that those over 65 whom were poor at the 60% mean income level and deprived were much more likely to score over the GHQ threshold. As with chronic illness though, is this propensity due to some other characteristic or can we isolate these economic factors as determinants of increased psychological distress? For instance, we have already seen that socio-economic status and chronic illness are related and both these variables are related to being female, thus could it not be that the effect of poverty is actually just an artifact of the composition of the elderly?

To try to separate out those factors that may confound the analysis, we enter the following variables into a model predicting a score greater than the GHQ threshold:

- *Age:* we have already seen that older people are more likely to be distressed.
- *Sex:* women consistently show higher levels of distress.
- *Marital Status:* Having a partner is known to decrease distress levels
- *Chronic Illness:* the last analysis showed that chronic illness has a large impact, thus a variable for this is also entered (as well as a variable to represent the degree to which the person is hampered in their day to day activities).

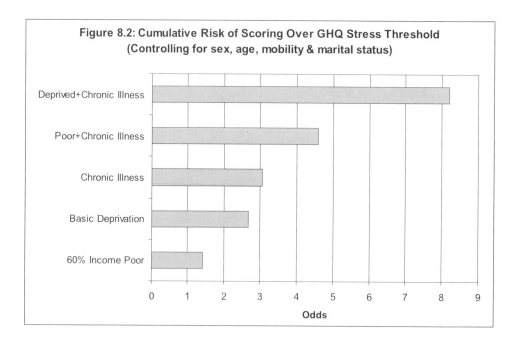

Figure 8.2: Cumulative Risk of Scoring Over GHQ Stress Threshold (Controlling for sex, age, mobility & marital status)

- *Income and Poverty:* after adding all these control variables into an equation, we then add variables that represent 60% income poverty and scoring one or more on the basic deprivation scale.

The last two variables are entered separately so that we can examine their effects in isolation and then together. To make interpretation easier, figure 8.2 shows the results of the equations in terms of the cumulative effect of the economic variables controlling for others that may confound their effect (the full model results are available in Appendix G).

The results in figure 8.2 show that, even controlling for a host of factors, including chronic illness and disablement, there is a significant effect for being either income poor or deprived on the basic index. When entered into an equation together, income poverty becomes insignificant, suggesting that basic deprivation is more strongly related to psychological distress. If we recall the results of Chapter 5, we have already seen that current income tends not to be a good predictor of current lifestyle among the elderly because of the impact of other influences such as savings and social networks. It is not surprising then that a direct measure of lifestyle such as basic deprivation is the more significant predictor. Individually however, both our poverty measures introduce a risk substantially smaller than that for chronic illness alone, underlining the impact of ill health on the well-being of elderly people. Of course, these factors often accompany one another, thus figure 8.2 shows how the risk of a psychiatric condition increases cumulatively if a person has several of the risk factors together. Being poor and having a chronic illness is highly associated with clinically significant levels of psychological distress. Whereas having a chronic illness alone leads to over three times the risk, in combination with income poverty the risk is four and a half times the odds of having neither of these factors. Similarly, if an elderly person is deprived and has a chronic illness this increases their risk of experiencing clinically significant levels of psychological distress to over eight times that of an elderly person with neither of these risk factors.

Conclusion

This chapter has examined the psychological health profile of those aged over 65 in the 1997 Living in Ireland Survey using the General Health Questionnaire and has compared the elderly to those aged under 65. A basic analysis of the GHQ by age and sex showed that women are more likely to have higher levels of distress than men and that there was a definite age progression in distress levels. It seemed at first that this heightened risk of distress was due to the levels of chronic illness among the elderly, but a more fine-grained analysis showed that younger groups with a chronic illness had similar levels of distress. In fact, the answer seemed to be that chronic illness among the elderly effected them in a different manner to younger groups and this explained the disparity. Decreased mobility seemed to be a particular problem among elderly people with a chronic illness compared to younger groups as did the impact of chronic illness on their daily activities (analysis not shown). The last chapter may suggest one particular reason for this since it showed that the chronic illnesses of the elderly were more likely to be of the musculo-skeletal or circulatory system whereas among younger respondents, skin diseases or emotional problems were more common. Although serious, the latter would affect mobility less severely.

Continuing the chief interest of this report, the final part of the chapter examined the impact of income and deprivation poverty on psychological distress. Results showed those over 65 who were in 60% income poverty had almost 1.5 times the risk and those in basic deprivation well over twice the risk of exceeding the GHQ threshold. However, in combination with a chronic illness (itself an outcome of deprivation as shown in the last chapter) chronic illness and deprivation led to almost 8 times the risk of psychiatric disturbance compared to an elderly person with none of these characteristics. As the last chapter showed, almost 45% of those aged over 65 have a chronic illness thus this has a very significant impact on the elderly population. 25% of the elderly population have a chronic illness in combination with income poverty, and this leads to 4.5 times the risk of developing a of psychiatric disorder compared to an elderly person with neither of these characteristics.

CHAPTER NINE

Social Interaction and Participation

Over the last decade or so the concept of 'social exclusion' has gained increasing prominence as the focus of research on the intersection of labour market insecurity and social marginality (Kronauer, 1998). One of the main concerns of this research has been to examine groups who through detachment from the labour market, possibly in conjunction with low income suffer social isolation from mainstream society (Paugam, 1991). This description sounds eerily close to the position of the elderly, who tend not to work, have low incomes (as shown in chapter 3 of this report) and are commonly found in single person households, yet the available evidence suggests that the social lives of elderly people are as rich, complex and variable as for other sections of the population (Fahey and Murray, 1994, pp.112-114; Whelan and Vaughan, 1982). However, the elderly are not an undifferentiated group and it is probable that some groups may suffer isolation because of particular characteristics. One such characteristic may be income, or material resources which are not sufficient to maintain social contacts, either because the individual cannot afford transport, or because deprivation and perceived stigma has led to social withdrawal. This chapter will examine the evidence in the 1997 Living in Ireland Survey on the extent of social contact and participation among elderly people in Ireland and how this varies by particular characteristics.

As discussed at length in Fahey & Murray (1994, p98-104), the demographic profile and family networks of those over 65 in Ireland contribute to a heightened risk of social isolation. The generations born in Ireland in the first 30 years of the twentieth Century had an exceptionally high incidence of non-marriage such that in the 1991 Census of the Population 20.4% of women and 24% of men in the age range 75-79 (birth cohort of 1911-1915) had never married. Five years later, the 1996 Census Report shows that 75-79 year olds had a slightly greater probability of having married (19.2% of women and 23.6% of men remaining single), a development which continues right through to cohorts born in the 1940's, but Ireland still has a high rate of non-marriage in comparison to other countries. As spouses and family networks form the primary webs of social integration, this pattern has important consequences for social interaction.

Another very important influence mentioned by Fahey & Murray on the kinnetworks of older people is migration. High levels of emigration from Ireland and migration within Ireland between rural and urban areas throughout the last century has meant that family networks are dispersed and children are quite likely to live at some distance form their parents. However, the children of the elderly in this study should have been relatively less prone to emigration as the vast majority would have entered adulthood after the 1950s at a time when emigration was dropping sharply.

With this demographic background in mind, we can now go on to examine the household structure of those aged over 65 in the 1997 Living in Ireland Survey.

Household Size and Structure

The household provides the most basic, but perhaps most important social network within which we live. Yet, a cursory glance across household statistics in the OECD countries shows that people are increasingly living alone, particularly in old age. As with marriage rates though, Ireland has a lower rate of single households among the elderly in comparison to other countries, a pattern that is set to continue in the near future as the cohorts of increasing marriage rates in the middle of the twentieth century continue into old age. We can get a better grasp of the household position of elderly people in table 9.1 which shows the proportions of people aged over 65 living in different types of households in the 1996 Census. These figures show that the proportion of elderly people in single households was 28.3% in 1996, a comparatively low figure when compared to other OECD countries, but still up from 24% in 1991 (Fahey & Murray, 1994)

Table 9.1: Proportions of Elderly in Various Types of Private Households

Household Type	% of Persons Aged Over 65
Single person households	28.3
Couples	25.7
Couple with children (any age)	12.8
Woman with children	6.4
Man with children	1.6
Couple with others (not children)	3.7
Not immediate family, but related (e.g. siblings)	8.0
Non-family, not related	2.5

Source: Census 1996, Volume 3, Table 9 p36.

Table 9.2: Living Arrangements of Those Aged 65+ In the 1997 Living In Ireland Survey

Household Type	% Men Aged:			% Women Aged:			
	65-69	70-79	80+	65-69	70-79	80+	All 65+
Elderly Person Alone	20.4	24.5	29.8	29.4	43.9	55.1	34.5
Elderly Couple	19.0	46.0	53.6	35.0	30.4	26.1	34.0
Elderly With Other Adults, No Children	57.9	27.0	15.5	32.5	20.5	15.2	28.2
Elderly With Other Adults, With Children	2.7	2.5	1.2	3.1	5.1	3.6	3.4
Total	100	100	100	100	100	100	100

Over a quarter of elderly people live in households made up of an elderly couple and almost 21% live with their children either as a couple or as a single person. Overall nearly 70% of people aged over 65 in private households live with some form of kin relation.

Table 9.2 shows the proportions of those aged over 65 in the 1997 Living in Ireland Survey in different household types by sex and age group. Table 9.2 shows that the proportion of single person households among the elderly grows larger as age increases in keeping with the earlier death of male partners. This pattern is confirmed by the larger proportion of men who live with their spouses compared to women (the proportion of men aged 65-69 in a couple is distorted by the presence of wives aged less than 65).

These figures suggest that the overall majority of elderly people are not isolated at the household level, although living with kin does not always guarantee positive relationships. Nonetheless, by far the largest proportion of care for the elderly happens via kin (O'Conner and Ruddle, 1988).

Social Interaction
Having seen that elderly Irish people are less likely than over 65s in other countries to live alone and moreover, quite likely to live among kin, what patterns of social interaction do they have with people outside of the household? The Living in Ireland Survey contains a number of items which ask about frequency of contact with different types of people as well as information on membership of clubs or organizations that can give us an insight into patterns of sociability among over 65s and what characteristics are associated with social exclusion.

Table 9.3: Frequency of Talking with Neighbours by Sex Among Over 65s

| | Sex | | |
	% Men	% Women	% All Elderly
Most days	71.9	58.8	64.6
1-2 times a week	21.3	33.4	28.1
1-2 times a Month	3.2	4.0	3.7
Less than once a month	2.6	2.7	2.6
Never	0.9	1.1	1.0
Total	100	100	100

Table 9.3 shows the proportions talking to neighbours by frequency of contact and sex. Contact here can be by telephone or face to face, but the answers to the question reveal an interesting differential by sex. Almost 72% of men state that they would speak to neighbours almost every day whereas more than 10% less women believe they have this frequency of contact. However, if we add together the categories for 'most days' and 1 to 2 times a week it is clear that there is actually very little difference between the sexes.

Similarly, table 9.4 shows that in terms of contact with friends or relatives 'who are not living in your household' at least once or twice a week, men have roughly the same levels of sociability as women. Almost 96% of men see friends or relatives at least once or twice a week compared to 92% of women. On the

Table 9.4: Frequency of Meeting Friends and Relatives by Sex Among Over 65s

| | Sex | | |
	% Men	% Women	% All Elderly
Most Most days	73.2	63.5	67.8
1-2 times a week	22.4	28.0	25.5
1-2 times a Month	2.6	5.9	4.5
Less than once a month	1.4	0.6	0.9
Never	0.5	2.0	1.3
Total	100	100	100

other hand, men have a significantly higher (P>.001) probability of stating that they meet friends or relatives on most days of the week. This difference is interesting as we could speculate that the higher rate of seeing friends and relatives among men may be because these men require domestic support given their limited prior experience of domestic work. The visitors may thus actually be carers, as well as social callers. However, although the gap between single men and women in terms of this form of sociability is greater than among men and women living in elderly couples, it is still significant in the latter[1] which suggests that aid from family and friends may be part of the discrepancy, but cannot totally explain the difference. Traditionally, men have usually socialized outside the home more in pubs and clubs (as we will see later in this chapter), thus this may also be the source of the sex differential.

The corollary of these figures is that there is a significant minority of elderly people, 4% of men and 8% of women, who meet friends or relatives less than weekly, although a further 2.6% of men and almost 6% of women meet family or friends at least once or twice a month.

Such figures reiterate the picture from the opening tables of quite high levels of social contact among elderly people, but how does this vary by household type? Are levels of sociability as high among single elderly people? Table 9.5 suggests that over 94% of people over 65 in single person households will talk with neighbours at least once or twice a week.

Table 9.5: Frequency of Talking with Neighbours by Household Type Among Over 65s

	Household Type			
	% Single Elderly	% Elderly Couple	% Elderly with Non-Elderly	% All Elderly
Most days	63.3	68.5	61.9	64.6
1-2 times a week	31.1	23.5	29.7	28.0
1-2 times a Month	2.1	3.6	5.5	3.7
Less than once a month	2.1	3.9	1.9	2.6
Never	1.5	0.6	1.0	1.0
Total	100	100	100	100

[1] Elderly men are significantly more likely than their wives to say that they see friends or relatives most days but this does not explain the differential.

Table 9.6: Frequency of Meeting Friends and Relatives by Household Type Among Over 65s

	% Single Elderly	% Elderly Couple	% Elderly with Non-Elderly	% All Elderly
Most days	69.2	70.8	63.0	67.8
1-2 times a week	25.3	23.5	28.2	25.6
1-2 times a month	1.8	4.2	7.2	4.4
Less than once a month	-	1.5	1.3	0.9
Never	3.7	-	0.3	1.3
Total	100	100	100	100

If anything, those elderly in households with non-elderly people talk with neighbours less, although the difference between the groups is not significant. Similarly, table 9.6 shows that single elderly people are the most likely to meet with friends or family at least once or twice a week. This might suggest that either single elderly are proactive in making contact with others to compensate for their position, or vice-versa. We have no information here either way, but some form of compensatory process does seem to occur.

How do rural elderly people fair in terms of social interaction? Living in a rural location may contribute to social isolation because of the relative weakness of

Table 9.7: Frequency of Talking with Neighbours by Location Among Over 65s

	Location								
	% Rural			% Urban			% All		
	Men	Women	All	Men	Women	All	Men	Women	All
Most days	76.4	52.5	63.5	67.7	64.1	65.7	71.9	59.0	64.7
1-2 times a week	19.2	42.2	31.6	23.3	26.5	25.1	21.3	33.5	28.1
1-2 times a month	2.9	4.1	3.5	3.6	3.9	3.8	3.2	4.0	3.7
Less than once a month	1.0	1.2	1.1	4.0	3.6	3.8	2.6	2.5	2.5
Never	0.5	0.0	0.2	1.3	1.9	1.7	0.9	1.1	1.0
Total	100	100	100	100	100	100	100	100	100

**Table 9.8: Frequency of Meeting Friends and Relatives
by Location Among Over 65s**

| | Location | | | | | | | | |
| | % Rural | | | % Urban | | | % All | | |
	Men	Women	All	Men	Women	All	Men	Women	All
Most days	71.6	59.0	64.7	75.0	67.1	70.3	73.3	63.5	67.7
1-2 times a week	23.6	34.0	29.1	21.3	23.1	22.3	22.4	28.0	25.5
1-2 times a month	3.8	4.1	4.2	0.9	7.5	4.7	2.4	5.9	4.5
Less than once a month	1.0	0.8	0.9	1.9	0.3	1.2	1.4	0.6	1.0
Never	0.0	2.0	1.1	0.9	2.0	1.6	0.5	2.0	1.3
Total	100	100	100	100	100	100	100	100	100

public transport systems compared to urban areas and because housing density falls make it less likely that one will see friends and neighbours.

Tables 9.7 and 9.8 list the responses to the questions already examined, but this time responses are divided by location and sex. Table 9.7 shows that although rural people over 65 are slightly less likely to speak with neighbours on a daily basis, this is not significant and they are in fact slightly more likely than urban dwellers to talk once or twice a week. There is also a much greater difference between men and women in rural locations compared to urban locations in terms of daily contact. However, table 9.7 shows that it is the high number of contacts 1-2 times a week among rural women which pushes up the overall count for this frequency of contact among rural respondents as a whole.

On the other hand, table 9.8 shows that rural elderly are significantly less likely to see friends and family on a daily basis which suggests that rural lifestyles may degrade these contacts slightly. Overall however, if we add together the two top categories again, there is little difference between the sociability patterns of the over 65s in rural and urban locations. Once again, there are much larger differences between men and women in rural areas compared to urban with rural women much less likely to see friends and family daily, but more likely to see them 1-2 times a week.

In terms of what we could call 'primary' socialization then, the overwhelming majority of elderly people have high levels of contact with people outside of their households. But does this sociability spread more widely? That is to say, do

Table 9.9: Proportion Who Are Members of a Club or Organization by Age Group, Sex and Location

Age Group	% Rural			% Urban			% All		
	Men	Women	All	Men	Women	All	Men	Women	All
17-30	54.9	41.0	48.2	60.5	30.8	45.6	58.6	34.2	46.5
31-50	51.6	34.4	42.5	55.7	42.3	49.0	54.3	39.2	46.6
51-64	45.1	30.7	39.1	54.6	39.6	46.8	50.2	36.4	43.6
65-69	25.4	27.5	26.2	52.6	40.7	46.2	39.2	34.8	36.9
70-79	23.4	12.6	17.6	34.9	32.4	33.5	29.5	23.6	26.2
80+	15.9	12.7	14.0	22.5	11.0	15.0	19.3	12.4	14.5
All Under 65	51.1	36.0	43.7	57.4	37.3	47.3	55.0	36.8	45.9
All 65+	22.6	16.8	19.5	38.7	29.7	33.5	30.9	23.9	27.0
All Ages	46.6	32.4	39.5	55.4	36.2	45.6	52.0	34.8	43.2

the elderly participate in organizations or clubs in the community? This type of social participation indicator is a little more difficult to interpret than the two previously analyzed since we are assuming here that elderly people want to be a member of 'organizations' and that this covers most forms of organized socialization. The question asks about membership of sports or social clubs and political parties, but it is fairly clear that the church or the pub, etc., may be far more important sources of social contact.

Table 9.9 shows the proportions who are members of a club or organization by age group, sex and location. Looking across the rows in table 9.9, men are significantly more likely than women to be members of organizations or clubs in all age groups and irrespective of location, apart from in rural locations among younger elderly people (those aged 65-69). There is some evidence that this gap closes with age, but it is interesting to note that, even after age 80, there is also a clear age gradient to membership with the older age groups being significantly less likely to be a member. In one sense, this is perfectly understandable given that older people are less likely to play the sports they may have done in their youth and thus will be less likely to be in a club overall. Nevertheless, it also suggests that elderly people do not replace membership of clubs that are no longer worthwhile with new affiliations.

Although living in a rural location does not seem to seriously limit social interaction with neighbours or friends and relatives it may well be a more significant factor in membership of a club or organization. Whereas family and neighbours may be relatively nearby, organizations tend to be in population centers and these will not always be easily reached from rural locations. Table 9.9 shows that those in rural locations are much less likely to be members of a club or organization, although as with the difference by sex, the gap closes in the eldest age group. In the two 'younger' elderly age groups on the other hand, the proportion in urban locations are almost twice those of rural elderly.

Social Participation and Material Resources
Given the differences that we have seen in the membership rates of rural and female elderly people, it seems apt to raise the possibility that these patterns may be due to lack of resources as well as geographical and social differences. That both of these groups were significantly poorer than general in Chapter 3 only adds to these suspicions. One basic test of whether income has an impact on membership of a club or organization is to look at the proportions split by income poverty at the 50% mean household level. However, we would get confounding effects from the interaction of older age, income and membership. To avoid this, tables 9.10 and 9.11 look solely at elderly between the ages of 65 and 69 divided by poverty, sex and location.

In fact, when we look at tables 9.10 and 9.11, the picture is rather complex as poor men have a lower probability of membership, whereas poor women's probability is higher (though neither of these differences is significant due to the small number of cases: N=310).

Similarly, table 9.11 shows that whereas there is very little difference in the probability of membership between the rural poor and non-poor, in urban areas the poor seem more likely to be members of a club or organization (although not significantly so).

Table 9.10: Proportion of Those Aged 65-69 Who Are a Member of a Club or Organization by Whether Poor at 50% Mean Income Level By Sex

| | 50% Mean Income Level | | |
	% Not Poor	*% Poor*	*% All*
Men	41.2	32.4	39.2
Women	31.6	42.6	34.8
All Elderly	36.7	37.5	36.9

Table 9.11: Proportion of Those Aged 65-69 Who Are a Member of a Club or Organization by Whether Poor at 50% Mean Income Level By Location

	50% Mean Income Level		
	% Not Poor	% Poor	% All
Rural	26.7	23.1	25.7
Urban	44.1	51.2	45.8
All Elderly	36.7	37.5	36.9

These bivariate analyses reveal a quite complicated relationship between income and social participation that suggests that we may be seeing the impact of other, as yet unmeasured variables. To make sure we are getting at the nub of the problem we need to control for other factors whilst investigating the relationship. Membership of clubs or organizations could also be seen as a fairly unrepresentative indicator of whether income impacts on sociability, thus the last part of this chapter investigates the impact of income on the measures used earlier in the chapter, *viz*, talking to neighbours and meeting friends and relatives. To control for other factors that may confound the analysis we need to use a model.

Within the model, we control for the basic demographic variables age and sex. More importantly, it may be that some of the variables we have already examined become significant in the analysis thus being in a rural location and living alone are entered. Frequency of contact may be restricted by chronic illness, or rather its direct effect on mobility, thus having a mobility problem is entered into the model. In a similar, though opposite fashion, being a member of a club or organization may be a positive influence on contact thus this is also controlled for.

Finally, we enter the variable of interest to us in this section of the chapter: whether the person has a low income. Based on earlier analyses we choose the 50% income poverty line as most elderly households were above the 40% line in chapter 3 and only a small proportion above the 60% income line. Table 9.12 gives the results of the models on the two frequency of contact questions. For ease of interpretation I have simply shown the full result for different age groups of elderly people when these groups are poor since this is our chief interest (the full results for the ordered logit model used can be found in Appendix H).

After controlling for a number of factors (see above), table 9.12 shows that income effects different types of contact in different ways. Low income actually

Table 9.12: Coefficient for the Effect of Age and Income Poverty on Two Types of Social Contact *(Controlling for Sex, Household Type, Location, Mobility Problems & Membership of Club or Organisation)*

	Talking To Neighbours	Meeting Friends or Family
Aged 65-69 AND 50% Income Poor	1.61***	0.17
Aged 70-79 AND 50% Income Poor	0.14***	-0.75***
Aged 80+ AND 50% Income Poor	0.7*	-0.26*

Key: ***=P<0.001 **=P<0.01 *=P<0.05

has a positive effect on contact with neighbours, although this effect reduces with age. On the other hand, income poverty has a negative effect on contact with friends and family, but only after age 69. These results are interesting, particularly in combination with tables 9.10 and 9.11 as they suggest that low income actually increases social contact, but only where this is *possible*. Thus in table 9.11, the urban poor were actually more likely to be members of clubs than non-poor whereas there was a slight decrease among rural poor. Could this be because the rural poor do not have organizations within easy reach like their urban cousins? Similarly, do the elderly poor substitute social contact for more expensive leisure pursuits, but only where their age allows? This would explain why contact with neighbours does not diminish and why younger poor elderly can still maintain links with family and friends.

Conclusions

This chapter has examined the household structure, social participation and social interaction patterns of the elderly. Social exclusion among the elderly has been a major concern of elderly interest groups and academics alike, but previous evidence has suggested that the elderly are not at any greater risk of social isolation than the general population. The results in this chapter tend to concur with this. In terms of their primary social support in the household, elderly people are less likely to live alone in Ireland than in most other countries in the OECD and likely to live among kin. In terms of contact with those outside the household, data from the Living in Ireland Survey shows that elderly men and women in Ireland have quite high levels of contact with both neighbours and friends and relatives. One would suspect that this optimistic picture would not hold if we examined sociability by household type. However, single elderly people appeared no more likely to have low levels of interaction with people outside the household. If anything, levels of interaction were higher for this group suggesting some form of compensatory mechanism was at work.

On the other hand, there did seem to be a real cost in terms of social interaction associated with living in a rural location. Compared to elderly people in urban areas, there was a significant decrease in the proportion in rural areas having daily contact with friends, relatives and neighbours. Similarly, we could observe a quite severe difference in rates of membership of clubs or organizations in rural areas compared to urban areas that suggests that the physical location makes quite a difference to patterns of social participation. Given the large difference in membership rates of clubs and organizations between men and women however, physical location cannot be the sole determinant. Within each age group women were much less likely than men to be a member, although the differential falls with age. We can see then that social and physical factors have an impact on patterns of social participation, but following the main theme of this report, the final section of the chapter examined the relationship between social interaction and material circumstances in terms of income. The differential between men and women and rural and urban dwellers in terms of club membership and frequency of contact had strong resonance with chapter three where we saw quite large differences in income levels between these groups. The question is, does income level impact on social participation among the elderly? The final analyses of the chapter showed that there is a relationship between income and interaction, but it is far from simple. Descriptive analyses showed that those under the 50% income poverty line were more likely to be members of a club, but only among women. Among men, poverty made membership less likely. To unwrap the relationship between income and social participation, we used a model to examine the impact of income poverty on the two indicators of frequency of contact. After controlling for a number of different characteristics we found a surprising result: income poverty and age where actually positively related to the frequency of social contact with neighbours, but there was a negative relationship between income poverty and the two older age groups and contact with friends and family. Could it be as suggested that elderly people substitute contact with neighbours and friends and family for more expensive leisure pursuits but only where their age permits? There certainly seems to be evidence for this in the patterns in the final table of the chapter.

CHAPTER TEN

Policy Implications and Recommendations

Introduction

The purpose of this chapter is to draw out the policy implications of the present study and make recommendations on issues affecting the living standards and well-being of older people. As indicated in the introduction, the study was carried out in the light of the National Anti-Poverty Strategy (NAPS) adopted by the Irish government in 1997. The chapter begins by recalling the policy context provided by the NAPS and the directions which the NAPS indicated that the present study should take. It then identifies some key findings of the study which are particularly relevant from a policy point of view, especially those that bear on the NAPS. Following on from that, the chapter takes up the question of income support for older people. It assesses the adequacy of social welfare pension provision in securing elderly people against poverty and makes recommendations on the future structure and levels of social welfare pensions. The chapter then turns to other dimensions of older people's well being, of which housing and health and social care are the most important.

Policy context

Two elements of the NAPS particularly informed the present study. The first was the NAPS global poverty-reduction target which advanced a core definition and measure of poverty (one based on low incomes *and* basic material deprivation). This provided the central concept of poverty which the study should aim to measure and a poverty-reduction target against which policy could be evaluated.

The second important feature of the NAPS was the broader, multi-dimensional definition of poverty within which the core concept of poverty just mentioned was presented. In this broader concept, the NAPS conceived of poverty as exclusion and marginalisation from 'participation in activities which are considered the norm for others in Irish society' (Government of Ireland 1997, p. 3). It pointed to many things, broadly under the headings of 'cultural, social and material resources', the lack of which could constitute dimensions of poverty. The NAPS provided a certain amount of elaboration of what this broader concept might mean in practice and on that basis identified a list of poverty

129

reduction targets while policy should aim to achieve. That elaboration of the concept in some instances pointed to concerns which were generic to all social groups (such as effective service delivery – though even in this case the services which would be relevant would vary from group to group). In other instances, however, it highlighted concerns which were more group-specific, and which in particular were of limited relevance to the elderly. Thus, for example, the NAPS focused considerable attention on unemployment and other labour market issues, and on education conceived of as a means of access to the labour market and other life chances. It did not refer to sub-groups such as the elderly for whom labour market issues would have little direct relevance, nor did it set out what should be taken as the parallel dimensions of poverty in their case.

This posed the challenge for the present study of exploring what the broad concept of poverty might mean in the case of the elderly. What are the functional parallels to such things as unemployment as a source of social marginalisation in the lives of the elderly? How important is current income as a dimension of elderly poverty? How much importance should we attach to such things as social isolation, poor health services, or inappropriate housing as contributors to social marginalisation among older people? While it would be unhelpful for policy purposes to come up with an exhaustive, unwieldy list of answers to these questions, it did seem necessary to identify the dominant ways in which the elderly could be disadvantaged and marginalised, over and above those associated simply with the lack of material resources.

Key findings
The key policy-relevant findings of the study can be broadly summarised as follows:

1. Current cash incomes among the elderly are generally low, with the result that many elderly fall below income poverty thresholds as traditionally defined. About 30 per cent of elderly-headed households have incomes below 50 per cent the national average, while almost six out of ten have incomes below 60 per cent of the national average.

2. However, measured against the core concept of poverty defined by the NAPS (low income plus material deprivation), the elderly are much less disadvantaged than they appear on the basis of income alone and are no worse off than the general run of the population. Just under 10 per cent of elderly-headed households are poor in NAPS terms, the same proportion as for the rest of the population. This level of poverty, though less extreme than would be suggested by income indicators alone, is still significant. It indicates that, in the case of the elderly, anti-poverty policy faces a considerable challenge if it is to achieve the NAPS target of reducing the poverty rate below 5 per cent by the year 2007.

3. The wide divergence between income poverty and NAPS poverty in the case of the elderly reflects the distinctively weak link between current cash income and material deprivation among older people. While current cash income is an imperfect indication of living standards among many social groups, the correlation between the two is particularly weak among older people – the elderly in general have higher living standards than their modest incomes would lead one to expect.

4. There are many reasons why the link between current cash incomes and the risk of material deprivation is weak among older people. Firstly, most elderly benefit from a range of 'free schemes' (state-provided benefits in kind) which are not available to the rest of the population (free travel, free electricity, free telephone allowance, etc.) and which are generally omitted in calculations of older people's current incomes. Some of these benefits are unevenly distributed among the target population (particularly in the case of free travel, which is of little value to those, such as rural dwellers, who have limited access to public transport), but generally they are progressive in being directed at the less well off. If valued in cash terms, they would add on average about 13 per cent to the incomes of older people and would significantly improve their income position relative to the rest of the population. Secondly, many elderly have accumulated significant resources which help sustain their living standards and reduce their expenditure requirements (e.g. most elderly own their homes outright and do not have rent or mortgage payments to make; many have accumulated household durables which are sufficient for their needs). High medical card coverage among the elderly population should be recognised as a further source of the weak linkage between income and living standards among older people.

5. Though the elderly are less poor than narrow income data would suggest, there are sub-groups in the elderly population whose incomes are particularly low compared to the rest. By far the highest risk category in this regard are those on Non-contributory Widows Pension, though the absolute size of this group is small. Those on Non-contributory Old Age Pension and Contributory Widows Pension also have elevated risk of income poverty, and since the absolute numbers in these categories are large, they account for the largest portion of the income-poor elderly.

6. Women are over-represented among those in the income categories just mentioned, and rural women are particularly over-represented. Income poverty among older people is thus feminised to a considerable degree, and is especially prevalent among rural elderly women. This in part reflects low rates of female participation in insurable employment in the past and the non-participation of the self-employed – of which farmers account for a large portion – in the social insurance system until recently.

131

7. While certain categories of the elderly population are clearly at higher risk of income poverty than others, the significance of this pattern has to be interpreted in the light of the weak link between low incomes and material deprivation among the elderly which has been noted above. Even those elderly with a distinctively elevated risk of income poverty (compared to the general run of older people) do not consistently show a correspondingly elevated risk of material deprivation, indicating that the intervening factors mentioned earlier are active in their case also. This is not to say that low incomes are unimportant as an indicator of disadvantage and hence a concern for anti-poverty policy, but that cash incomes are less crucial as a means of alleviating elderly deprivation than is the case for other sectors of the population.

8. Of the additional dimensions of poverty which affect older people, one important cluster relates to housing. While many older people are well off in housing terms (in that they live in good houses which they own outright), many others (even many of those who own their houses) have serious housing problems. While problems of this kind can affect all categories of the population, the present study has found (Chapter 4 above) that they are especially salient among older people. The most common housing problem experienced by older people consists of poor physical housing standards, as caused by such things as dampness, rotting external timber-work and poor heating. Older people in private rented accommodation are especially likely to have problems of this kind (and they may also be exposed to insecurity of tenure and rent increases which would increase the vulnerability of this particular sub-group). Further problems may have to do with the material suitability of the house to the changing needs of older people whose health or mobility is declining, and the location of the house, particularly in the case of rural elderly who live away from service centres and lack transport.

9. A further major set of factors which could be considered an important dimension of disadvantage for certain categories of older people concerns health and social care services. The transition to ill-health and/or physical dependency is a traumatic one in the lives of older people. Well-being and quality of life in the aftermath of that transition are crucially affected by the quality and availability of health and social care services. The consequence is that where such services are unavailable, are excessively costly or are of poor quality, older people who need them can experience profound deprivation. Inadequacies in health and social care services, and in particular the poor level of development of community-based services for frail and dependent elderly, are thus a major source of disadvantage for certain categories of the elderly population.

10. Though health and health-related services can be considered as distinct dimensions of disadvantage for older people, they are linked to other dimensions and especially to low incomes and material disadvantage. Poor health is reciprocally related in the long-term to social disadvantage and deprivation – social deprivation helps cause health disadvantage, and poor health in turn worsens the risk of social disadvantage over the life-course (for example, by impeding labour market success). Inadequate access to health and social care services is also in large part a function of income inequality. The less well-off cannot afford to purchase the health insurance which will provide them with access to private medical care and therefore depend on the public health system where waiting lists, overcrowding and other inadequacies in the health services (especially in regard to hospital services) are concentrated. While the public health system meets many of the health-service needs of the less well-off elderly who depend on it, deficiencies in that system bear down most heavily on those with low incomes and low levels of other material resources and so add to their relative disadvantage.

Policy implications

From a NAPS point of view, one broad implication of the present study is the need to refine and elaborate the NAPS concept of poverty so that it relates more effectively to the circumstances of major sub-groups of the population such as the elderly. This implication relates not so much to the core indicator of poverty based on the combined income plus deprivation measure, as this indicator is as relevant to the elderly as to any other population segment. It relates rather to the additional dimensions of disadvantage which the NAPS highlights in its broader characterisation of poverty. Though the elaboration of these additional dimensions in the NAPS is valuable for the attention it draws to the multi-dimensional nature of poverty, it is limiting in its focus on issues (such as unemployment and early education) which are of little direct relevance to the elderly and which therefore do little to illuminate those dimensions of life which can lead to severe disadvantage for certain segments of the elderly population. Housing and health-related issues are particularly important in this regard and these will be referred to further below.

Income maintenance

Cash income has a less clear-cut significance for poverty among the elderly than it has for the rest of the population since it is only weakly related to deprivation among older people. This means in many instances that the relief of elderly deprivation may not be efficiently tackled by marginal increases in elderly cash incomes, since a large proportion of the total cost of such increases would go to older people who are not deprived. It also means that for anti-poverty policy to focus solely on the raising of minimum cash income levels among the elderly may be somewhat misdirected – it may impose large costs on the exchequer while at the same time it may fail to address certain forms of deprivation among older people.

At the same time, however, there is no denying that income poverty and income maintenance are important for older people – not as important, perhaps, as they might first appear but not to be underrated either. Furthermore, income maintenance provisions are at present at the heart of the government's response to elderly poverty. For policy purposes, therefore, it is worth devoting considerable attention to the question of income maintenance, with particular reference to present government commitments in this regard.

The £100 per week pension
Present government policy on income maintenance among older people is centred on the commitment negotiated as part of the present programme for government to raise the old age pension to £100 per week by the year 2002. This commitment arises in the context of a consensus which has emerged since the late 1980s that future income provision for older people should rest on a two-pillar system (for the most recent and most complete articulation of this consensus, see Pensions Board, 1998). The first pillar consists of social welfare pensions, the function of which is to provide what the Pensions Board refers to as the 'minimum retirement income guarantee', that is a floor income below which no elderly person should have to fall. It is not intended that this first pillar should apply universally to all old people, since there are and may continue to be some elderly who are outside the social insurance system while at the same time have sufficient means not to qualify for social assistance pensions (and therefore to have incomes from their own resources which keep them above the floor income). However, it is intended to apply to the vast majority of older people.

The second pillar consists of voluntary occupational or other private pensions which can be thought of as top-ups to social welfare pensions which individuals may choose to secure for themselves during their working lives. These are financed as part of the individual's remuneration package in pre-retirement employment, or through personal purchase of a private pension plan during the person's working life. Their function, taken in conjunction with 'first pillar' pensions, is to provide retired people who secure them with an income proportional to their pre-retirement income. It is now an accepted principle of policy that as many people as possible should be encouraged to make such second pillar provision for themselves and thus improve the ratio between post-retirement and pre-retirement income for future generations of older people.

In this context, the commitment to a £100 per week social welfare pension for older people relates to the 'minimum retirement income guarantee' and so at first

**Table 10.1. Pensions Payment Rates (Maxima per Week)
for Older People, 1999/2000**

	Rate per week	Differential with Contrib. Old Age Pension
Contributory Old Age/Retirement Pension	£89.00	–
Non-contributory Old Age Pension	£78.50	–11.7%
Contributory Widow(er)s Pension (aged 66 or over)	£82.10	–7.7%
Non-contributory Widow(er)s Pension (aged 66 or over)	£78.50	–11.7%

Source: Department of Social, Community and Family Affairs

sight would seem to amount to a target floor income for older people which the government has committed itself to achieving by the year 2002.

What does the £100 per week pension mean?
Though the commitment to a £100 per week old age pension at first sight appears straightforward, its precise significance needs some teasing out. This is so in part because the commitment does not in fact specify *which* old age pension it is intended to raise to £100 per week – the contributory/retirement pension or the non-contributory pension[1]. Nor does it make explicit reference to the pensions for widow(er)s, which also form a major part of social welfare provision for older people. This amounts to a considerable ambiguity, since the range of pension schemes for older people entails a range of payment levels and it is a matter of some moment which of those levels is intended to reach £100 per week by the year 2002 (see Table 10.1).

In practice, the Department of Social, Community and Family Affairs, which has responsibility in this area, has taken on to implement the government's commitment by reference to the *top* social welfare pension for older people, that is, the Contributory Old Age Pension (and its adjunct, the Retirement Pension). Payment levels for these now stand £89 per week (compared to £78 per week in 1997), and so are to be raised by a further £11 per week to reach the £100 target by 2002.

According to the Living in Ireland Survey, about 40 per cent of elderly households received that top pension in 1997, while over 50 per cent received

---

[1] The contributory old age pension and retirement pension, though having slightly different entitlement criteria, are set at identical levels of payment and for simplicity will be referred to here as contributory old age pensions).

pensions with lower levels of payment (28 per cent received the Non-contributory Old Age Pension, 21 per cent received the Contributory Widows Pension and 4 per cent received the Non-contributory Widows Pension). These proportions are changing over time, in that the balance of coverage is steadily shifting towards contributory schemes and away from non-contributory schemes (for example, the number of recipients of non-contributory old age pensions declined by a fifth between 1988 and 1998, while recipients of contributory-based pensions increased by a similar proportion).[2] The significance of the differentials in payment levels between the higher and lower old age pensions is thus gradually declining since an ever-increasing proportion of the elderly population is shifting onto the higher pension.

Yet the numbers on the lower pension payments are still large and will remain so for a considerable time. In consequence, the differentials between the various pension payments continue to be important for anti-poverty policy. The differential between the top and bottom pension payments (that is, between the Contributory Old Age Pension and the basic Non-contributory Old Age and Widows Pensions) stands at 11.7 per cent at present, and 7.7 per cent in the case of Contributory Widows Pensions (Table 10.1). The Pensions Board (1998), following the Commission on Social Welfare (1986), recommended that the maximum differential should be reduced to 10 per cent, though the National Pensions Board in 1994 had recommended that the differential should be eliminated altogether, as resources permit (National Pensions Board 1994, pp. 126-7).

Under present arrangements, therefore, *the commitment to a £100 per week pension by the year 2002 is in fact a commitment to a range of pension payments of which £100 per week is the upper bound.* The lower bound is not specified, but if the recommendations of the Pensions Board in 1998 and the Commission of Social Welfare in 1986 on this question were adopted, *the lower bound would be £90 per week in 2002.* The Contributory Widows Pension, which at present is in an intermediate position between these upper and lower bounds, is not referred to in the commitment, and there is no independent guide to indicate what relative levels it may be expected to reach in 2002.

Thus to assess the adequacy of the government's commitment on old age pensions by the year 2002, the payment level to be kept in mind is not only the £100 per week upper bound, but also the £90 per week lower bound which that

---

[2] The increase in contribution-based pensions is due to economic growth, the growing participation of women in the workforce, the extension of social insurance to new categories of the workforce (such as the self-employed in 1988 and part-time employees in 1991) and the relaxation of contribution conditions for eligibility for contributory pensions.

commitment appears to entail, along with the intermediate payments level which may be associated with the Contributory Widows Pension.

The role of non-cash benefits

Before turning to an assessment of such adequacy, a further complication to be kept in mind is the role of non-cash benefits provided by the 'free schemes' available to the elderly (free travel, free television licence, etc). These amount to a large social welfare expenditure programme, which cost £109 million in 1997 (excluding the cost of medical card coverage). If averaged out over the recipient elderly population, they would add about 13 per cent to their cash incomes (the inclusion of an imputed value for medical card coverage would add further to those incomes). Discussion of adequate levels of pension provision for older people to date have not taken account of these non-cash benefits. The £100 per week old age pension target for 2002 has been set without reference to them. This distorts discussion to some extent, since those benefits have a real and very large cost and may be presumed to have a correspondingly large impact on elderly living standards. Though this has not been explicitly stated, the presumption at present must be that the old age pension target for 2002 (upper bound, as mentioned above) is £100 per week *plus* free schemes, with lower-payment pensions enjoying free-scheme add-ons of a similar scale.

Is the target adequate?

The target pension for 2002 set out by government represents a 5.1 per cent annual rate of growth in the top old age pension payment for the period 1997-2002. Since inflation at present is running at less than 2 per cent per annum and is not projected to increase substantially for the foreseeable future, this rate of growth will undoubtedly give rise to a substantial increase in *absolute* (as opposed to relative) income levels among older people.

The extent to which it alters the relative income position of older people will depend on the rate of growth in average national household income over the period, since this is the reference point against which relative income is measured. Given the performance of the economy in the recent past and the reasonably favourable projections for the future, a nominal annual growth rate of 5 per cent in average household income, or a real annual growth rate of 3 per cent (assuming 2 per cent annual inflation), is quite attainable. In any event, the rate of real growth in average national household income is unlikely to be significantly less than the rate of growth in old age pension income implied by the government's pension target for the year 2002. *Therefore it is unlikely that the government's old age pension target for 2002 will radically alter the relative income position of older people by that year.* It may be enough to prevent a deterioration in the income position of older people, but it is unlikely to be enough to bring about an improvement. *In consequence, it is unlikely to have a substantial effect on the risk of relative income poverty among older people.*

Looking at this question from a slightly different point of view, the Pensions Board has recently suggested that the government's pension target for the year 2002 is too low (Pensions Board 1998, p. 87). The Board judged that an upper-bound old age pension of £99 per week would have been necessary in 1998 in order to provide a minimum adequate income for older people, implying considerably higher levels of increase in old age pensions than the government had envisaged. This conclusion was arrived at on the basis of the Commission on Social Welfare (1986) estimates of minimum adequate incomes, as uprated for the 1990s by Callan *et al.* (1996). The latter uprating proposed basic social welfare rates in the range £68 – £96 per week as minimum adequate rates. The Pensions Board felt that, in the case of the elderly, the upper edge of that range – £96 per week in 1996 terms – would represent an appropriate minimum (the Board did not set out in detail why it chose the upper edge rather than a point lower down the range as appropriate for the elderly – Pensions Board 1998, p. 87). This was equivalent to 34 per cent of average industrial earnings in 1996. The actual post-Budget old age pension (contributory) in 1998 was the equivalent of 28.5 per cent of average industrial earnings in that year. *The Board recommended that the government should aim over the next 5-10 years to raise the top old age pension payment to the level of 34 per cent of average industrial earnings, a level of increase which, on the basis of its projections, the Board found to be considerably higher than that implied by the government's target for the year 2002.*[3]

Consistency in social welfare payments

While the Pensions Board argued that the government target for old age pensions is too low and has recommended considerably larger increases over the next 5-10 years, other commentators have queried the basis on which the elderly should be singled out for special treatment in government targets for social welfare

---

[3] Note that the Pension Board's reference point in assessing the adequacy of old age pension payments relative to incomes for other categories is average industrial earnings (AIE), which is the average gross income of workers in manufacturing industry as measured annually by the CSO's Census of Industrial Production. The corresponding reference point adopted by the National Anti-Poverty Strategy, by contrast, is average household disposable income (AHDI), which referrs to disposable incomes among all households, as measured by the Living in Ireland Survey. Since AHDI is a more comprehensive population measure and refers to disposable rather than gross income, it is a more useful reference point in assessing income adequacy than AIE. It is important also to note that, in recent years, AHDI has grown much faster than AIE – the former increased by 22 per cent between 1994 and 1997, while AIE increased by only 8 per cent. The differential arises mainly because the AHDI (a measure of disposable income) takes account of income tax cuts where the AIE (a measure of gross income) does not, and the AHDI takes account of economic sectors (especially services) where income growth was faster than in manufacturing industry. This is not to say that, in the future, AHDI will continue to grow faster than AIE (a return of income tax increases, for example, would favour growth rates in AIE over AHDI).

increases. Though the details of these queries vary, the common thread is a concern that special treatment for the elderly may breach the principle of consistency in social welfare provision. This principle, as enunciated by the Commission on Social Welfare, lays down that, as far as possible, equivalent needs and circumstances should be dealt with in the same fashion in the social welfare system (Commission on Social Welfare 1986).

Expressing a concern of this type, the Combat Poverty Agency has argued that social welfare provision for old people is now moving ahead more rapidly than for other social welfare recipients and is widening the gap between old age pensions and other social welfare payments (Combat Poverty Agency 1999, p. 4). In the Agency's view, while the social welfare increases for older people introduced in the 1999 Budget (which amounted to £6, or 7.2 per cent, in the case of Contributory Old Age Pension) will help to reduce the numbers of older people who are consistently poor, it could give rise to a situation where welfare categories with equivalent needs are treated differently and this could have the effect of some people appearing to be treated as 'more deserving' than others (Combat Poverty Agency 1999, p. 4). From the point of view of the NAPS, the Agency felt that such an approach would be contrary to a coherent strategic approach to poverty alleviation, since the obvious strategic requirement would be to focus most effort on the worst-off categories. Disproportionate increases in old age pension increases were out of line with that requirement: 'Put bluntly, money spent in this manner, while reducing the risk of poverty for older people, may have had a greater anti-poverty effect if spent on a larger increase to the lowest social welfare payments, so reducing the number of recipients who were consistently poor' (Combat Poverty Agency 1999, p. 4). In so far as the elderly may be judged to have special needs compared to other social welfare recipients, for example in the area of health and social care services, the Agency recommended that provisions targeted directly on those needs, such as medical cards or allowances related to a need for personal care, might be a more appropriate solution than a cash differential in social welfare payments related only to chronological age. In other words, in order to deal with the special needs of particular categories of older people, targeted supports given to directly to those with such special needs would be a more efficient response than a general increase in social welfare payments for all older people.

The representative of the Minister for Finance on the Pensions Board likewise raised concerns about excessive increases in old age pensions, in this instance in the context of dissent from the Board's proposed target rate for old age pensions of 34 per cent of average industrial earnings. Apart from the predictable Department of Finance concern about the public finance implications of the Board's recommendation, he queried whether levels of elderly poverty were such as to warrant pension increases of that scale and whether the elderly could be regarded as meriting more favourable treatment than other welfare categories (Pensions Board 1999, p. 118).

Recommendations on income maintenance for older people

Attempting to draw together the various considerations just outlined, the following recommendations on income maintenance for older people could be offered:

1. The target Contributory Old Age/Retirement pension rate of £100 per week for the year 2002 should be regarded as the minimum necessary to preserve the relative income position of older people, since it implies a rate of growth in elderly social welfare pension incomes that is likely only to keep pace with, and not exceed, growth in average disposable income for all households. It, therefore, should not be regarded as an exceptionally generous commitment likely to bring about a substantial improvement in the relative income position of older people (even though it will yield a real improvement in the absolute incomes of older people). Even taking the value of non-cash benefits into account (which would significantly improve the income position of the elderly relative to the national average), elderly incomes remain modest in general and are such as to leave a significant minority of older people in or on the margins of poverty.

2. Within its existing commitments regarding social welfare pensions up to 2002, the government could achieve a further significant reduction in elderly poverty by focusing on those pension payments which at present are implicitly targeted to reach less than £100 per week by 2002. These consist of the Non-contributory Old Age Pension and both the Contributory and Non-contributory Widows Pensions (which, if present relativities were to persist to 2002, would have payment rates ranging down to £90 per week, or perhaps less). Recipients of these latter pensions have a particularly high risk of poverty, and show high vulnerability on other dimensions also. This is particularly so in the case of rural elderly women, who comprise a large proportion of the recipients of these pensions. *A strong case could be made both on efficiency and equity grounds that the present differential between the payment rates for these pensions and those for Contributory Old Age pensions should be reduced by the year 2002, in the sense that the lower payments should be raised closer to the £100 per week target than is implied by present commitments.* The efficiency case in favour of such a move rests on the large impact on elderly poverty which it would have. The equity case rests on the gendered nature of the present situation, in that women comprise the bulk of those on the lower pension payments. This in turn is in part a reflection of women's past disadvantage in relation to

participation in insurable employment and so can be seen as a legacy of past social inequalities rather than a justifiable differential based on differential contributions to the social insurance system.

3. On the basis of certain assumptions about the composition of the elderly population in receipt of social welfare pensions in 2002 and about the differentials between the various levels of social welfare payment for older people which would otherwise prevail in that year,[4] full elimination of those differentials would add approximately 4 – 4.5 per cent to the total cost of social welfare pension payments (old age and widows) for older people in 2002.

4. Pension increases for the elderly are justifiable on the basis of the government's general poverty reduction targets, rather than on the basis that the elderly have special needs which warrant higher levels of social welfare payment than are received by other categories of the welfare dependent population. Given that pensions for older people are now more generous than social welfare payments for many other categories of the population, it has been suggested that they are in conflict with the principle of consistency within the social welfare system. That suggestion could be answered in any of three different ways: the first is to argue that the elderly have special needs which give rise to higher income requirements and thus mean that higher levels of old age pensions are justified on the basis of the principle of consistency; the second is to propose that old age pensions be made consistent with other social welfare payments by allowing them to fall to the levels of those other payments, while the third is to propose that other payments be raised to the levels of old age pensions. Taking these three answers in turn, the first is not justified by the facts, as there is no evidence that the elderly in general have income needs which exceed the norm for the rest of the population (though see 6 below). There is therefore no factual basis for arguing that special treatment of the elderly in the social welfare system is in keeping with the principle of consistency. The second option – reducing old age pensions to the levels of other social

---

[4] The assumptions are (a) that half of elderly social welfare recipients in 2002 would be on what at present are the lower pension payments (that is, a quarter on the lowest payments – Non-contributory Old Age Pension and Non-contributory Widows Pension – and a quarter on the somewhat higher payments associated with the Contributory Widows Pension); and (b) that the average differential between those lower payments and the top pension payments would be in the region 8–9 per cent (that is, that the largest differential, which would apply to the Non-contributory Old Age Pension and Non-contributory Widows Pension, would be 10 per cent, and the smallest differential, which would apply to the Contributory Widows Pension, would be of the order of 7-8 per cent, thus giving an average between the two of 8-9 per cent). As that differential would apply to about half of the elderly population in receipt of social welfare pensions, its elimination would add about 4-4.5 per cent to the total social welfare pensions cost.

welfare benefits – would lead to an increase in relative income poverty and the risk of deprivation among older people, while doing nothing to improve the position of other social welfare recipients. It thus would add to total poverty levels in the population and therefore would be contrary to present anti-poverty policy. By elimination, this leaves the third option – raising other social welfare payments to the levels implied by present commitments on old age pensions – as the approach which is most in keeping with both anti-poverty policy and the principle of consistency. The implication is that a consistent approach to social welfare payments, viewed in the context of present anti-poverty policy, would require government commitments in regard to old age pensions to be paralleled by similar commitments to other categories of social welfare claimants and not be taken in isolation. As this implication bears on central elements of government fiscal and expenditure policy, its signficance extends well beyond policy on older people. It therefore needs to be assessed in terms that go beyond the remit of the present report.

5. The question of indexing elderly pensions against an independent benchmark of changes in living standards has often been raised. The Pensions Board (1998), for example, recommended that social welfare pensions be indexed to average industrial earnings, with the top pension payment set at the level of 34 per cent of average industrial earnings. While there is no single scientifically correct solution on the question of indexation, the following observations can be made here:

   • Once social welfare incomes have been brought up to an adequate level, indexation against an indicator of mean national household income is technically effective as a means of preserving their relative position and thus preventing the re-emergence of poverty among the social welfare population. However, the substantive desirability of such a measure is dependent on a wide range of additional factors, having to do with overall government spending, the structure of the tax-benefit system, economic growth and so on. It thus amounts to a fundamental policy choice (and may be justifiable as such) rather than a narrow technical mechanism, and needs to be evaluated as such.

   • There is no particular justification for indexing old age pensions alone in the social welfare system. If indexation is to be introduced, the principle of consistency would require that it be extended widely through the social welfare system and not confined to a particular category of claimants.

   • If indexation of social welfare payments is to be pursued, average industrial earnings do not seem to offer a particularly good reference point to use for this purpose. That index is based on only a subset of workers (rather than all households) and refers to gross rather than net or disposable earnings. Ideally, the index chosen should bear as close a relationship as possible to changes in the living standards of all households. It therefore should represent all households and relate to disposable rather than gross income. These requirements do not point definitively to any particular index as the most desirable, since a number of options are possible, but they do serve to eliminate some of the indices which have are commonly referred to in this connection (such as the index of average industrial earnings and the consumer price index)

6. To the extent that certain categories of older people do have special needs (which arise mainly in connection with housing, health and social care), these should be met with measures directly targetted on those needs rather than through generalised increases in social welfare pensions directed at all elderly pension recipients.

Housing

Alongside incomes, housing emerged as a significant dimension of disadvantage for older people. Since *The Care of the Aged* report (1968), it has been repeatedly recognised that the provision of suitable housing can often be a key requirement for older people, especially where growing physical dependency threatens the older person's capacity to continue living in their own homes. In the three decades since *The Care of the Aged* report, housing standards among older people have improved immeasurably, as part of the general improvement in housing standards for the population as a whole. Reported satisfaction among older people with their housing circumstances has also improved over the years (Fahey and Murray, 1994). Yet problems remain, as the housing deprivation index examined in Chapter 4 above indicates. The proportion of the elderly who live in housing with substantial physical defects (dampness, wood rot, poor heating) is larger than for the rest of the population, and certain sub-categories, especially those in private rented accommodation, are in a particularly vulnerable position. There has been relatively little progress in housing provision which is specifically designed to suit the needs of older people or which incorporates the kind of assistive technology which would enable older people facing physical decline to maximise their quality of life in their own homes (Ruddle *et al.* 1997). As a result, some older people are likely to be struggling to cope in housing which no longer suits their health or mobility circumstances.

It must also be recognised, however, that, given the high rates of outright home ownership among the elderly, housing is a significant dimension of *advantage* for many older people. Older people's incomes are below the national average, but their wealth holdings (comprised mainly of housing assets) are above the national average (Nolan 1991, pp. 27-29). The rapid rise in house prices in recent years is likely to have yielded a large increase in the total wealth holdings of the elderly population. This more positive side of the housing picture for older people raises a number of questions for policy, two of which can be highlighted here. The first is how to enable older people to draw greater benefit from their housing wealth. This question is particularly important in the case of older people who may have low incomes and low standards of living even though they may own housing assets of considerable value.

The second question is how to cope with the equitableness of public transfers to a section of the population which may have real needs but which may also own large amounts of wealth. To date, debate on this question in Ireland has arisen largely in connection with the financing of long-term care for frail elderly people. In that context, the central equity problem is that state subvention of the cost of care (e.g. through health board subventions towards nursing home costs for eligible patients) may have the effect of preserving the assets of older people and thus increasing the estate they pass on to the next generation. The older person's heirs may thus turn out to be the main beneficiaries of state subventions in such cases, even though those heirs may already be quite well off. The inequity of such an outcome has given rise to considerable discussion on how the state might recoup some of the cost of the subvention from the older person's estate (for a good review of this issue, see O'Shea *et al.*, 1991, pp. 149-155). Similar problems could be said to arise in other areas of policy, for example, in the case of publicly-funded housing improvements for older people. These might be justified in the case of the older people themselves but the benefit might soon transfer to heirs who would have little claim to state largesse of that kind on their own account.

These considerations point to the complex range of policy issues which arise in connection with the housing circumstances of older people, taking account of both the positive and negative aspects of those circumstances. From an anti-poverty perspective, the first concern of policy must be to alleviate housing deprivation among those elderly who experience problems of poor physical housing conditions and who are unable to remedy those defects from their own resources. A range of policy instruments are already in use with that purpose in mind, consisting of various forms of provision of social housing and sheltered accommodation under the aegis of the local authorities, voluntary housing agencies and health boards. Services under these headings include not only the provision of accommodation but also various schemes for the repair and upgrading of older people's existing homes (such as the Essential Repairs Grants scheme and the schemes administered by the Task Force on Special Housing Needs for the Elderly).

Housing services for the elderly under these headings have recently been thoroughly examined and commented upon by the National Council on Ageing and Older People in its review of the implementation of *The Years Ahead* report (1988) (National Council on Ageing and Older People, 1997). Among the conclusions and recommendations arrived at in that review were following:

- The level of social housing provision for older people had declined in recent years.
- Needs assessment and planning in connection with social housing provision for the elderly in local authorities were inadequate and did not fulfill the recommendations of *The Years Ahead* report.
- Coordination between local authorities and health boards on the provision of sheltered and semi-sheltered accommodation for older people was underdeveloped (to the point where it usually did not exist at all) and the overall supply of such accommodation was limited.
- The planning and design of social housing for the elderly usually differed from standard housing only in that the dwellings were smaller. Little progress had been made towards the ideal of lifetime adaptable housing for older people and the incorporation of 'assistive technology' into housing design for physically impaired residents.
- Schemes for the repair and upgrading of older people's homes were reactive, fragmented and possibly underfunded – though in the absence of comprehensive assessment of need, it was not possible to to establish what level of funding and provision would be adequate.

Market solutions
In addition to social provision of housing for older people, market solutions are also often appropriate as a means to deal with at least some of the housing problems of the elderly. However, the policy context in which the housing market operates is often inimical to the effective operation of such solutions or promotes a less than optimal use of housing assets among older people. The most general indication of this is the underdevelopment of market provision of housing specifically targeted on the elderly (such as sheltered or semi-sheltered housing, a form of housing which is almost totally absent in the private market in Ireland). Even those older people who could afford to pay for housing specially tailored for their needs often find that the market does not respond and the range of options available to them is narrow or unsuitable.

Among the features of the policy environment which contribute to this narrowness in the housing market for older people are the following:

- Transaction costs in the housing market are high, arising in part from the high levels of stamp duty on the purchase of dwellings. These costs hamper residential mobility and thus give an incentive to older people to continue living in housing that may be inappropriate to their needs. It also discourages older people from 'trading down' to smaller dwellings as they age, thus releasing cash resources from their accumulated housing assets as the need may arise.

- Owner-occupied residential property, and thus the income-in-kind which arises from owner occupation, is untaxed, whereas virtually all other forms of income is taxed. This biases savings and investment towards owner-occupied housing and gives older people an incentive to retain their assets in the form of housing. This in turn hinders the liquidation of those housing assets in favour of alternative investment combinations which would yield a more appropriate mix of cash income and housing.

- The private rental property market is under-developed, particularly in connection with the law on tenant-landlord relations and security of tenure. As a result, rent rises are unpredictable and tenure in most tenancies is highly insecure. This discourages older people from considering private rental accommodation as a housing option, even though private renting might in some cases be more appropriate to their needs. It also hinders the emergence of private rental versions of the sheltered or semi-sheltered housing referred to earlier, even though in some instances such versions of sheltered housing might be attractive to certain categories of older people.

The combined effect of these features is to dampen market demand for certain kinds of housing provision, limit the variety of accommodation available in the market and thus restrict the range of housing options available to older people. However, these features of the private property market are deeply embedded in the policy environment and affect the fundamental character of the housing system as a whole. They are often positively valued because they promote high levels of home-ownership, relatively high levels of investment in housing as opposed other assets and long-term stable occupation of family homes. While these outcomes may be beneficial for certain categories of the population, they can be counter-productive for many older people. The latter might be better served by a housing system which would facilitate partial disinvestment in housing in favour of other income-producing assets, promote secure and easy-access rental tenure as well as difficult-access ownership tenure, and encourage residential mobility in response to changing needs rather than inflexible residential stability.

It is beyond the scope of the present report to make detailed recommendations on how such an improved balance in the housing system might be achieved, since the issues involved affect the entire housing system rather than just housing for the elderly. Nevertheless, it is important to highlight that these issues exist and warrant closer attention in the future development of anti-poverty policy for older people, as well as in overall debates on housing policy in Ireland.

Health and social care services

As in the case of housing, it has been long and widely accepted that adequate health and social care services are essential to older people's well-being. It has also often been pointed out – and reiterated in the present report – that social inequalities in access to health and social care services and in health itself run parallel to other inequalities. In particular, those who have low levels of material well-being are also likely to have worse physical health and psychological well-being and to have to rely on less than fully adequate public health services.

The detailed implications of this situation for health and social care policy for older people have been explored at length elsewhere, not least by National Council on Ageing and Older People (1997). It is not the place here to review those implications again. However, a number of key points can be made in the context of anti-poverty policy, and these are as follows:

- In considering the overall nature of poverty, the health dimension (which includes both health itself and the services provided to sustain health and cure illness) is of particular importance to older people, since the risk of ill-health rises sharply in old age. At the same time, the health dimension of poverty is not simply a concern for older people, since the links between poverty and poor health accumulate in a long-term and reciprocal fashion over the life-course. Poverty at younger ages (even in childhood) increases the risk of early onset of ill-health and of premature death; ill-health at younger ages increases the risk of poverty (for example, through restriction of labour market activity). A poverty-ill health linkage may in some cases arise solely in old age, but more typically it is likely to be the culmination of processes that originated well in advance of old age.

- Given the centrality of health to the well-being of older people, along with the cumulative, life-long nature of the linkages between poverty and ill-health, a strong case could be made for inclusion of health issues in future reviews of the NAPS. While these issues have greatest significance for older people, their rootedness in earlier stages of the life course would require that they be addressed for all age-categories of the population and so be treated as a poverty dimension for the whole population rather than for the elderly alone.

- Given the importance of health and social care services for elderly people, improvements in those services, especially in the publicly-funded sector, should be accorded an importance parallel to improvements in income maintenance in anti-poverty policy for older people.

- While a general high standard of provision in health and social care services is an essential interest of older people, it is important that a proper balance be struck between development of the high-technology, hospital based and institutional end of the care system on the one hand

and the community-based, low-technology, time-intensive end of the care system on the other. Since the 1960s, growth in the health services system has tended to concentrate on the former, whilst the development of the latter has been much slower. Thus, for example, whatever shortcomings may be present in the hospital care system, they would appear to be less extreme than the shortcomings in such things as the home help service, outpatient transport, day care, other domiciliary services and information provision. Likewise, developments in the private nursing home sector in the last ten years have greatly outstripped developments in home-based supports for older people (National Council on Ageing and Older People 1997). The result is that although health policy frequently enunciates the principle of 'ageing in place' (i.e. that older people as far as possible should be enabled to live in their own homes as they enter physical decline), the necessary services to achieve that end have been slow to develop and have tended to be overshadowed by developments in the field of institutionalised care. It is important for older people's well-being that a better balance be achieved in these areas in the future.

In the case of elderly health, as in the case of elderly housing, it is easy to adopt a policy focus which is too narrowly concentrated on the elderly themselves and neglects the broader context which links the elderly with the rest of the population. This is most obviously so in connection with mortality. The most disadvantaged elderly from a health point of view, it could be said, are comprised of those now-missing elderly who have died prematurely, either in the early years of old age or before they arrived at old age. The risk of being in that category is strongly linked to poverty and social disadvantage. All surviving elderly, therefore, could be considered at a certain advantage from the health point of view since they have escaped the mortality that has befallen a share of their contemporaries. They may well also have an advantage from a poverty point of view, since the most impoverished of their peers are likely to be over-represented among those who succumbed to early death. These are well-known and in some respects inescapable facts of life, but they do have the implication that both health policy and anti-poverty policy for the elderly should be placed in a life-course context. In the long-run, if the elderly are to receive maximum benefit, health policy should reach down the age-range and take account of those who would hope to be old one day as well as those who are already in that situation.

APPENDIX A

In 1987, it was found that when compared to external sources, the final sample of 3,310 households over represented the rural compared to urban households (the former tended to have a higher response rate than the latter), but under represented households headed by the under 35s or those headed by semi-skilled and unskilled manual workers. Lastly, the nature of the sampling frame meant that the sample under represented households with one or two adults compared to those with three or more. The reweighting of the sample sought to address these problems using four key variables: household location (urban/rural), number of adults in the household, occupation of the household head and the age of the head of household. Using information from the CSO, weights were calculated that re-balanced the survey population according to the Labour Force Survey for the year and 'grossed' the population up to the number in the total population in that year.

The problems of the 1994 survey were very similar to those in 1987 since the design of the survey was almost identical, but the procedure was augmented with a step to correct for the distribution of persons within households. Thus, after correcting for the proportion of small farm households, the sample was reweighted to take account of the over representation of rural households and under representation of households led by a younger person or one from an employed and manual occupation. With household weights constructed, the sample of individuals was weighted (by first adopting the weight constructed for the household) to take account of imbalances in the proportions of men and women, married, single, separated and widowed people and younger persons.

As already mentioned, the 1994 Living in Ireland Survey was the first wave of a panel survey, the fourth wave of which is used in this report to analyze the circumstances and lifestyle of elderly people in 1997. However, just as samples experience non-response in cross-sectional surveys, these problems are exacerbated in panel surveys which return to the same individuals each year. Although a great deal of energy and resources are used attempting to minimize the extent of non-response, or 'attrition' suffered by panel surveys, it is inevitable that some households or individuals will refuse to participate, be uncontactable, or become ineligible in successive years. Such attrition can lead to bias thus the sample needs to be reweighted to take account of any loses. Procedures were carried out to this effect following each wave after 1994. The 1997 Living In Ireland Survey was weighted by the following criteria to ensure representativeness.

Individual Characteristics

1) Age group (16-19, 20-24, 25-34, 35-44, 45-54, 55-59, 60-64, 65-70, 70-74, 75+) by sex.

2) Age group by marital status (Under 30, married, Under 30, Never Mar., 30-44, married, 30-44, never married, 45-64, married, 45-64, never married, Under 65, widowed, 65+, married, 65+, never married, 65+, widowed, All ages, separated/divorced) by sex

3) Economic Status (self-defined: Employee, Self-employed, Farming, Seeking 1st Job, Unemployed but as worked, Disabled, Retired, Home Duties, Education/training) by sex.

4) Socio-economic group (Agriculture/Fish. Etc., Professional/Managerial, Non-manual, Manual, NA) by sex.

5) Education (No qualifications, Lower Secondary, Upper Secondary, Third Level) by sex.

6) Receipt of social welfare payments (U.A. etc., U.B., OAP_C/Ret. Pen., OAPNC, PRETA, WID._C, WID_NC, LPA, CARER, D.B., I.P., DPMA)

Household Characteristics

7) Household Size (6 categories)

8) Number of adults in household (6 categories)

9) Number of elderly – age 65 or over – in household (none, one, 2 or more)

10) Number working 15+ hours in household (none, 1,2, 3 or more)

11) Urban/rural location of household in start wave (Dublin, Other Urban (10000+), Rural)

12) Poverty status of household in wave 1 (Scale A, 50% line)

13) Household equivalised income decile in wave 1

14) Net household income decile in wave 1

15) Whether household at same address in start wave and end wave

16) Whether members of the household formed new households at any time between 1994 and 1997.

Household 'Head' Characteristics (traditional patriarchal definition of head)

17) Sex of head

18) Age group of head (Under 25, 25-34, 35-44, 45-54, 55-64, 65+)

19) Marital status of head (Married, Separated/Divorced, Widowed, Never Married)

20) Economic Status (self-defined: Employee, Self-employed, Farming, Education/training, Unemployed, Disabled, Retired, Home Duties)

21) Socio-economic group of Head (Farming, Other Ag./Fishing, Higher Professional, Lower Professional, Employer/Manager, Salaried Employee, Intermed. Non-Man, Other Non-Man., Skilled Manual, Semi-Skilled Manual, Unskilled Manual, No Occupation/NS)

Following adjustment, the 1997 data is a representative sample of the Irish population that will produce results that can be generalized to the entire population.

Logistic Model of The Probability of Being Poor at the 50% Mean Income Level

Variable	Model 1	Model 2	Model 3	Model 4	Model 5
Household Head Aged <65	Ref. -	Ref. -	Ref. -	Ref. -	Ref. -
Household Head Aged 65-74	1.80 ***	1.79 ***	1.46 **	1.35 *	0.87 n.s
Household Head Aged 75+	1.50 **	1.46 **	1.09 n.s	0.90 n.s	0.29 ***
Urban		Ref. -	Ref. -	Ref. -	Ref. -
Rural		1.22 *	1.27 *	1.39 ***	1.23 *
Multi-Person Household			Ref. -	Ref. -	Ref. -
Single Person Household			1.99 ***	1.39 **	0.89 n.s
Male Head of Household				Ref. -	Ref. -
Female Head of Household				2.50 ***	1.75 ***
Relies on Non-Pension Income					Ref. -
Relies on Old Age Contributory Pension					1.47 n.s
Relies on Old Age Non-Contributory Pension					11.89 ***
Relies on Widows Contributory Pension					16.29 ***
Relies on Widows Non-Contributory Pension					48.32 ***
Relies on Occupational Pension					0.80 n.s
Constant	- ***	- ***	- ***	- ***	- ***
-2 Log Likelihood and Sig. F	2942.54 ***	2937.89 *	2899.37 ***	2836.31 ***	2660.83 ***

Key: ***=P<0.001, **=P<0.01, *=P<0.05, n.s=Non-Significant, 'Reliance'=66% or more of total disposable income.

APPENDIX C

Rotated Factor Solution for Life Style Indicators

Basic Dimension	Basic 1987	Basic 1997	Housing Services 1987	Housing Services 1997	Secondary 1987	Secondary 1997
A meal with meat, chicken or fish	0.59	0.49	0.22	0.29	0.24	0.11
A warm, waterproof overcoat	0.55	0.72	0.23	0.01	0.13	0.06
Two pairs of strong shoes	0.58	0.71	0.20	0.05	0.17	0.13
A roast joint of meat or its equivalent once a week	0.46	0.45	0.16	0.09	0.38	0.28
New, not second hand clothes	0.58	0.55	0.13	0.01	0.22	0.34
Go without a substantial meal	0.61	0.51	0.04	0.02	-0.05	-0.01
Go without heat	0.63	0.56	-0.10	0.02	0.12	0.05
Go into debt for ordinary living expenses	0.58	0.50	-0.10	-0.15	0.15	0.24
Housing/Services Dimension						
Refrigerator	0.07	0.02	0.44	0.75	0.07	0.05
Washing Machine	-0.02	-0.08	0.45	0.50	0.30	0.41
Colour TV	0.02	0.02	0.43	0.61	0.24	0.04
Dry, damp free dwelling	0.15	0.28	0.31	0.31	0.21	0.21
Non-shared indoor toilet	0.11	0.1	0.84	0.82	-0.13	-0.03
Non-shared bath or shower	0.11	-0.02	0.84	0.80	-0.09	0.13
Secondary Dimension						
Telephone	0.04	0.05	0.19	0.15	0.59	0.56
Car/Van	0.14	0.24	0.05	0.04	0.53	0.41
Weeks annual holiday away	0.08	0.17	0.04	0.03	0.68	0.72
Central heating	0.07	0.13	0.23	0.33	0.52	0.44
Be able to save regularly	0.17	0.14	0.10	0.05	0.58	0.67
Daily newspaper	0.18	0.04	0.09	0.07	0.52	0.46
Hobby or leisure activity	0.25	0.32	-0.08	-0.02	0.46	0.49
Presents for friends or family	0.32	0.39	0.08	0.19	0.48	0.39
Able to afford afternoon or night out	0.20	0.42	-0.03	-0.04	0.43	0.35

APPENDIX D

Table D.1: Logistic Model of the Probability of Being Deprived on the Basic Index (score > 0)

Variable	Odds	Sig
Main Terms:		
Household Head Aged <65	Ref.	
Household Head Aged 65-74	0.43	***
Household Head Aged 75+	0.33	**
Male Head of Household	Ref.	
Female Head of Household	1.40	*
Urban	Ref.	
Rural	0.62	***
Multi-Person Household	Ref.	
Single Person Household	0.95	
Interactions:		
HOH Aged 65-74 & Rural Location	1.66	
HOH Aged 75+ & Rural Location	4.56	***
Constant		***
-2 Log Likelihood and Cox & Snell R^2	2195.7	0.03

*Significance Key: *=<0.5, **=<0.01, ***=<.001.*

Table D.2: Logistic Model of the Probability of Being Deprived on the Secondary Index (score > 0)

Variable	Odds	Sig
Main Terms:		
Household Head Aged <65	Ref.	
Household Head Aged 65-74	1.19	
Household Head Aged 75+	0.78	
Male Head of Household	Ref.	
Female Head of Household	3.98	***
Urban	Ref.	
Rural	1.54	***
Multi-Person Household	Ref.	
Single Person Household	0.77	*
Interactions:		
HOH Aged 65-74 & Rural Location	2.39	***
HOH Aged 75+ & Rural Location	1.42	
HOH Aged 65-74 & HOH Female	0.30	***
HOH Aged 75+ & HOH Female	0.83	
Constant		***
-2 Log Likelihood and Cox & Snell R^2	3572.3	0.07

*Significance Key: *=<0.5, **=<0.01, ***=<.001.*

Table D.3: Logistic Model of the Probability of Being Deprived on the Housing Index (score > 0)

Variable	Odds	Sig
Main Terms:		
Household Head Aged <65	Ref.	
Household Head Aged 65-74	1.72	*
Household Head Aged 75+	2.93	***
Male Head of Household	Ref.	
Female Head of Household	0.85	
Urban	Ref.	
Rural	1.78	***
Multi-Person Household	Ref.	
Single Person Household	4.06	***
Interactions:		
HOH Aged 65-74 & Rural Location	0.90	
HOH Aged 75+ & Rural Location	0.27	***
Constant		***
-2 Log Likelihood and Cox & Snell R^2	1644.5	0.05

*Significance Key: *=<0.5, **=<0.01, ***=<.001.*

APPENDIX E

Logistic Model of Being Poor for the Combined Income and Deprivation Measure

Variable	Odds	Sig
Main Terms:		
Household Head Aged <65	Ref.	
Household Head Aged 65-74	0.71	
Household Head Aged 75+	0.47	*
Male Head of Household	Ref.	
Female Head of Household	1.40	*
Urban	Ref.	
Rural	0.57	***
Multi-Person Household	Ref.	
Single Person Household	1.02	
Interactions:		
HOH Aged 75+ & Rural Location	5.03	***
Constant		
Improvement in Zero Slopes G2 and Cox & Snell R^2	1692	0.02

Significance Key: *=<0.5, **=<0.01, ***=<.001.

APPENDIX F

Logistic Model of The Probability of Having a Chronic Illness Over 65s

Variable	Model 1 Odds	Sig.	Model 2 Odds	Sig.	Model 3 Odds	Sig.	Model 4 Odds	Sig.
Man	Ref.	-	Ref.	-	Ref.	-	Ref.	-
Woman	1.52	**	1.44	*	1.52	**	1.48	**
Aged 65-69	Ref.	-	Ref.	-	Ref.	-	Ref.	-
Aged 70-79	1.95	***	1.76	***	2.34	***	2.17	***
Aged 80+	1.91	***	1.91	**	2.35	***	2.29	***
Urban	Ref.	-	Ref.	-	Ref.	-	Ref.	-
Rural	0.94	***	0.95	n.s	0.81	n.s	0.86	n.s
Multi-Person Household	Ref.	-	Ref.	-	Ref.	-	Ref.	-
Single Person Household	0.73	*	0.63	**	0.75		0.64	**
Highest Education:								
Tertiary	Ref.	-	Ref.	-	Ref.	-	Ref.	-
No Quals	1.31	n.s	1.17	n.s	0.95	n.s	0.83	n.s
Junior Cert. Equiv.	1.38	n.s	1.15	n.s	1.23	n.s	0.94	n.s
Leav. Cert. Equiv.	1.59	n.s	1.58	n.s	1.32	n.s	1.25	n.s
Poor			1.16	n.s	1	n.s	0.95	n.s
Deprived on Basic Index			2.31	***			23.01	**
Deprived on 2ndary Index					2.15	***	2.14	***
Both Basic & 2ndary Dep.							0.07	*
Constant		***		***		***		***
N	1070		1006		1005		989	
-2 Log Likelihood and Sig. F	1285.39	***	1200.23	***	1196.78	***	1137.37	***

Key: ***=P<0.001, **=P<0.01, *=P<0.05, n.s=Non-Significant.

APPENDIX G

Logistic Model of Reaching the General Health Questionnaire Clinical Threshold Among Over 64s

	Model 1		Model 2		Model 3	
Variables	*Odds*	*Sig.*	*Odds*	*Sig.*	*Odds*	*Sig.*
Aged 65-69	Ref.	-	Ref.	-	Ref.	-
Aged 70-79	1.25	n.s	1.24	n.s	1.24	n.s
Aged 80+	3.11	***	3.21	***	3.11	***
Man	Ref.	-	Ref.	-	Ref.	-
Woman	1.34	n.s	1.37	n.s	1.30	n.s
Chronic Illness	3.06	***	3.20	***	2.92	***
Degree to Which Chronic Hampers Daily Activities:						
No Problems	Ref.	-	Ref.	-	Ref.	-
Some	1.62	n.s	1.67	n.s	1.74	n.s
Severe	6.19	***	5.05	***	6.28	**
Marital Status:						
Married and Living Together	Ref.	-	Ref.	-	Ref.	-
Widowed	0.98	n.s	0.90	n.s	0.94	n.s
Single	0.86	n.s	0.97	n.s	0.80	n.s
Deprived on Basic Index	2.68	***			2.48	***
Poor at 60% Mean HH Income			1.43	*	1.34	n.s
Constant		***		***		***
N	1004		944		944	
-2 Log Likelihood & Sig. Of F	831.2		769.4	***	767.22	***

Key: ***=P<0.001, **=P<0.01, *=P<0.05, n.s=Non-Significant.

159

APPENDIX H

Ordered Logit Model of Frequency Meeting Friends and Relatives

	Estimate & Significance			
	Model 1		Model 2	
Woman	0.02	n.s	0.03	n.s
Aged 65-69	0.09	n.s	0.08	n.s
Aged 70-79	-0.23	*	0.01	n.s
Aged 80+	-0.39	**	-0.43	*
Single Person Household	0.12	n.s	0.19	n.s
Rural Location	-0.22	***	-0.22	***
Have Mobility Problems	-0.69	***	-0.66	***
Member of Club or Organization	0.23	***	0.24	***
50% Income Poor	0.07	n.s	0.17	*
Aged 65-69 AND 50% Income Poor			-0.07	n.s
Aged 70-79 AND 50% Income Poor			-0.92	***
Aged 80+ AND 50% Income Poor			-0.01	n.s
Log Likelihood	-4891.46		-4883.59	

*Key: ***=P<0.001, **=P<0.01, *=P<0.05, n.s=Non-Significant N: 6584.*

References

Bartley, M. and Plewis, I. (1997) Does Health-Selective Mobility Account for Socio-Economic Differences in Health? Evidence from England and Wales, 1971 to 1991. *Journal of Health and Social Behaviour* **38**, 376-386.

Bowling, A. (1991) *Measuring Health. A Review of Quality of Life Measurement Scales*, Milton Keynes: Open University Press.

Bowling, A., Grundy, E. and Farquhar, M. (1997) *Living Well Into Old Age: Three Studies Of Health And Well-Being Among Older People In East London And Essex*, London: Age Concern.

Callan, T., Nolan, B., Whelan, B.J., Hannan, D.F. and Creighton, S. (1989) *Poverty Income and Welfare in Ireland*. 146, Dublin: ESRI.

Callan, T., Nolan, B. and Whelan, C.T. (1993) Resources, Deprivation and the Measurement of Poverty. *Journal of Social Policy* **22**, 141-172.

Callan, T., Nolan, B., Whelan, B.J., Whelan, C.T. and Williams, J. (1996) *Poverty in the 90s: Evidence from the 1994 Living in Ireland Survey*, Dublin: Oak Tree Press.

Cavelaars, A. (1998) *Cross-National Comparisons of Socio-Economic Differences in Health Indicators*. Erasmus University. Doctorate.

Combat Poverty Agency (1999) The National Anti-Poverty Strategy and the 1999 Budget, *Poverty Today Supplement*, April/May.

Crimmins, E.M., Hayward, M.D. and Saito, Y. (1994) Changing Mortality and Morbidity Rates and the Health Status and Life Expectancy of the Older Population. *Demography* **31**, 159-175.

Cunny, K.A. and Perry, M. (1991) Single Item Vs Multiple-Item Measures of Health Related Quality of Life. *Psychological Reports* **61**, 127-130.

Davey-Smith, G., Blane, D. and Bartley, M. (1994) Explanations for Socio-Economic Differentials in Mortality: Evidence from Britain and Elsewhere, *European Journal of Public Health*, **4**, 132-144.

Elstad, J.I. (1998) The Psycho-Social Perspective on Social Inequalities in Health. In: Bartley, M., Blane, D. and Davey Smith, G., (Eds.) *The Sociology of Health Inequalities*, pp. 39-58. Oxford: Blackwell

Fahey, T. and Murray, P. (1994) *Health and Autonomy Among the Over-65s in Ireland.* 39, Dublin: National Council for the Elderly.

Farquhar, M. (1995) Elderly People's Definitions of Quality of Life. *Social Science and Medicine* **41**, 1439-1446.

Fox, A.J. (1989) *Health Inequalities in European Countries*, Aldershot: Gower Publishing.

George, L.K. and Bearon, L.B. (1980) *Quality of Life in Older Persons: Meaning and Measurement*, New York: Human Sciences Press.

Goldberg, D. and Williams, P. (1988) *A User's Guide to the General Health Questionnaire*, Windsor: NFER-Nelson.

Honohan, P and Nolan, B. (1993), *The Financial Assets of Households in Ireland*, 162, Dublin, ESRI.

Kazis, L.E., Anderson, J.J. and Meenan, R.F. (1989) Effect Sizes for Interpreting Changes in Health Status. *Medical Care* **27**, S178-189.

Kelly, S., Hertzman, C. and Daniels, M. (1997) Searching for the Biological Pathways Between Stress and Health. *Annual Review of Public Health* **18**, 437-462.

Kronauer, M. (1998) 'Social Exclusion' and 'Underclass' - New Concepts for the Analysis of Poverty. In: Andress, H.J., (Ed.) *Empirical Poverty Research in Comparative Perspective,* Aldershot: Ashgate.

Kuh, D.J.L. and Ben Shlomo, Y. (1997) *Lifecourse Approach to Chronic Disease Epidemiology*, Oxford: Oxford University Press.

Lundberg, O. (1991) Childhood Living Conditions, Health Status and Social Mobility: A Contribution to the Health Selection Debate. *European Sociological Review* **7**, 149-162.

Mack, J., Joanna, L., Lansley, G. and Steward, H. (1985) *Poor Britain*, London: Allen & Unwin.

Markides, K.S. (1993) Trends in the Health of the Elderly in Western Societies. In: Atkinson, A.B. and Rein, M., (Eds.) *Age, Work and Social Security*, London: Macmillan.

Marmot, M.G., Kogevinas, J. and Elston, M.A. (1987) Social/Economic Status and Disease. *Annual Review of Public Health* **8**, 111-135.

Marmot, M.G. and Wadsworth, M.E.J. (1997) *Fetal and Early Childhood Environment: Long Term Implications*, Edinburgh: Churchill Livingstone.

Mheen, H.v.d., Stronks, K., Looman, C.W.N. and Mackenback, J.P. (1998) The Role of Childhood Health in the Explanation of Socio-Economic Inequalities in Early Adult Life. *Journal of Epidemiology and Community Health* **52**, 15-19.

Moffit, R. (1989) Estimating the Value of In-Kind Transfer: the Case of Food Stamps. *Econometrica* **57**, 385-409

Nolan, B. (1991) *The Utilisation and Financing of Health Services in Ireland.* 155, Dublin: ESRI.

Nolan, B., Callan, T., Whelan, C.T. and Williams, J. (1994) *Poverty and Time: Perspectives on the Dynamics of Poverty.* 166, Dublin: ESRI.

Nolan, B. and Whelan, C.T. (1996) *Resources, Deprivation and Poverty,* Oxford: Clarendon Press.

Nolan, B. and Cantalon, S. (1998) Are Married Women More Deprived Than Their Husbands? *Journal of Social Policy* **27**, 151-171.

O'Boyle, C., McGee, H., Hickey, A, O'Malley, K. and Joyce, C.R.B. (1992) Individual Quality of Life in Patients Undergoing Hip Replacement, *Lancet,* 339, 1088-1091.

O'Cinneide, S. (1972). The Extent of Poverty in Ireland, *Social Studies,* **1 (4),** 381-400.

O'Conner, J. and Ruddle, H. (1988) Caring for the Elderly, Part II: The Caring Process: A Study of Carers in the Home, Dublin, National Council for the Aged.

O'Shea, E., Donnison, D. and Larragy, J. (1991), *The Role and Future Development of Nursing Homes in Ireland,* Dublin: National Council for the Elderly.

Pahl, J. (1983) The Allocation of Money and the Structuring of Inequality Within Marriage. *Sociological Review* **31**, 235-262.

Pahl, J. (1989) *Money and Marriage,* London: Macmillan.

Paugam, S. (1991) *La disqualification Sociale: Essai Nouvelle sur la Pauverté,* Paris: PUF.

Ringen, S. (1987) The *Possibility of Politics,* Oxford: Clarendon Press.

Rottman, D. (1994) Allocating Money Within Households: Better Off Poorer? In: Nolan, B. and Callan, T., (Eds.) *Poverty and Policy in Ireland,* Dublin: Gill and Macmillan

Ruddle, H., Donoghue, F. and Mulvhill, R. (1997) *The Years Ahead Report: A Review of the Implementations of Its Recommendations,* No. 48, Dublin: National Council on Ageing and Older People.

Townsend, P. (1979) Poverty *in the United Kingdom,* Harmondsworth: Penguin.

Townsend, P. and Davidson, N. (1982) *Inequalities in Health (The Black Report),* Middlesex: Penguin.

Wadsworth, M.E.J. (1986) Serious Illness in Childhood and its Association With Later Life Achievement. In: Wilkinson, R.G., (Ed.) *Class and Health: Research and Longitudinal Data*, London: Tavistock.

Whelan, B.J. and Vaughan, R.N. (1982) *The Economic and Social Circumstances of the Elderly in Ireland*. 110, Dublin: The Economic and Social Research Institute.

Whelan, C.T., Hannan, D.F. and Creighton, S. (1991) *Unemployment, Poverty and Psychological Distress*. 150, Dublin: ESRI.

Wilkinson, R.G. (1996) *Unhealthy Societies: The Afflictions of Inequality*. London: Routledge.

National Council on Ageing and Older People

The National Council on Ageing and Older People was established in March 1997 in succession to the National Council for the Elderly (January 1990 to March 1997) and the National Council for the Aged (June 1981 to January 1990).

The functions of the Council are as follows:
1. To advise the Minster for Health on all aspects of ageing and the welfare of older people, either at its own initiative or at the request of the Minister and in particular on:

   (a) measures to promote the health of older people;
   (b) measures to promote the social inclusion of older people;
   (c) the implementation of the recommendations contained in policy reports commissioned by the Minister for Health;
   (d) methods of ensuring co-ordination between public bodies at national and local level in the planning and provision of services for older people;
   (e) methods of encouraging greater partnership between statutory and voluntary bodies in providing services for older people;
   (f) meeting the needs of the most vulnerable older people;
   (g) means of encouraging positive attitudes to life after 65 years and the process of ageing;
   (h) means of encouraging greater participation by older people;
   (i) whatever action, based on research, is required to plan and develop services for older people.

2. To assist the development of national and regional policies and strategies designed to produce health gain and social gain for older people by:

   (a) undertaking research on the lifestyle and the needs of older people in Ireland;
   (b) identifying and promoting models of good practice in the care of older people and service delivery to them;
   (c) providing information and advice based on research findings to those involved in the development and/or implementation of policies and services pertaining to the health, well-being and autonomy of older people;

(d) liaising with statutory, voluntary and professional bodies involved in the development and/or implementation of national and regional policies which have as their object health gain or social gain for older people.

3. *To promote the health, welfare and autonomy of older people.*

4. *To promote a better understanding of ageing and older people in Ireland.*

5. *To liaise with international bodies which have functions similar to the functions of the Council.*

The Council may also advise other Ministers, at their request, on aspects of ageing and the welfare of older people which are within the functions of the Council.

MEMBERSHIP

CHAIRMAN   Dr Michael Loftus

Mr John Brady	Ms Janet Convery
Mr John A Cooney	Mr Jim Cousins
Mr Joseph Dooley	Cllr Michael Finnerty
Mr James Flanagan	Ms Margaret Geary
Dr John Gibbon	Prof Faith Gibson
Mr Frank Goodwin	Dr Mary Hynes
Mr Eamonn Keane	Ms Betty Keith
Ms Sheila Kennedy	Mr Jack Killane
Ms Leonie Lunny	Ms Mary McDermott
Dr Diarmuid McLoughlin	Ms Mary Nally
Mr Pat O'Leary	Ms Mary O'Sullivan
Mr Peter Sands	Ms Sarah Scott
Mr Bernard Thompson	Mr Liam Walsh
Dr Margo Wrigley	

DIRECTOR	Mr Bob Carroll
RESEARCH OFFICER	Dr Nuala O'Donnell
COMMUNICATIONS OFFICER	Mr John Heuston
PROJECTS OFFICER*	Vacant

*Ms Trish Whelan is currently on a career-break.